THE ROGUE'S GUIDE TO THE JEWISH KITCHEN

For Gorgi, Big Hip and Little Hip

THE ROGUE'S GUIDE TO THE JEWISH KITCHEN

A Feast of Yiddish Foods for Thought and Eating

Daniel Rogov
David Gershon
David Louison

Illustrations by Lise Norwick

THE JERUSALEM POST
& CARTA / NITZANIM BOOKS

ISBN 965-220-070-0

Phototypeset by Astronel
Plates by Tafsar
Printed by Chen
All in Jerusalem, Israel

CONTENTS

LIST OF RECIPES
(in the order in which they appear in the text)

Foreword

THE THREE AUTHORS of this little book are, at least in our own eyes, an interesting collection. Rogov, a social critic who takes nearly everything too deeply to heart, protects himself by lovingly attacking and chuckling at nearly all of those institutions which are held sacred by men and women; Gershon, the true gourmet of the group, thrives primarily on those aspects of life that appeal to the senses; and Louison, the most casual of us, enjoys following those aspects of the world that keep it ticking but never quite allow it to explode.

We have, since we first met on a small Greek island, collaborated on six books. In that time we have, despite our differences, come closer and closer together and enjoy nothing better than sitting over long meals or extended coffees and talking about everything of interest to civilized human beings. Politics, art, philosophy, literature and the cinema are favourite topics but by far our time is most heavily invested in discussions concerning food and eating. We may or may not be oral types, but we leave that to our readers, including the psychoanalysts among them, to decide.

In some ways we are quite different, one from the other. One of us comes originally from a small village in Russia; one is an expatriate New

York American; and the other is an urban Israeli. One is an inveterate cinema buff, another finds his joy in an ongoing study of that esoteric branch of philosophy known as rational metaphysics (whatever that may be), and the third devotes his excess energies to dogs, garden and Georges Simenon novels.

We share commonalities as well. Although none of us practices religion in an orthodox manner we are all what might be called "very Jewish" in that we thrive on the ethical, cultural and historical aspects of our Judaism. We particularly enjoy reminiscences about our varying Jewish backgrounds. Whether it was in New York, Mogilev or Tel Aviv, we all had Jewish mothers, fathers and grandparents who influenced our lives and life-styles enormously. On comparison we are frequently amazed at how similar were our pasts. We speak and understand Yiddish at various levels but each of us enjoys spicing his speech with Yiddishisms and, despite any other arguments about our Jewishness, we all admire Woody Allen.

And we each have a special place, both in our hearts and on our palates, for Jewish food. Although each of our kitchens boast several specialties, we frequently feature those foods that we consider most "our own" — those of the Yiddish kitchen.

We also share a special warmth for Lise Norwick, a good friend who has illustrated each of our books. Lise, a young Englishwoman who resides in Greece, has never failed to delight us with her imagination and ability to capture the precise flavour of what it is that we are trying to say. Lise, in a phrase, understands us.

The essays found throughout the book, although they may sometimes poke a bit of fun at just about everything, should not be taken wrongly. They are written and presented with love. For those, however, who disagree with our commentaries, each essay has been initialled by its author, and readers may decide on their own where praise or condemnation is in order. As to the selection, preparation and sampling of the recipes, that was done jointly. Not at all a bad way to make a living.

Daniel Rogov
David Gershon
Tel Aviv, 1984   David Louison

Introduction

It is difficult to know whether there are more jokes about Jewish mothers, Jewish food or kosher chickens . . .

Mel Blanc

IF ONE WANTS to give thanks for the advent of what we today consider Jewish food, it is to Nebuchadnezzar, the somewhat schizophrenic king of ancient Babylonia that such kind thoughts should be addressed.

Jews had been long settled in Israel before the Babylonian invasion of 587 B.C.E. and although the dietary laws of the Old Testament had taken firm root among the people, *matzoh* and *mannah* do not a national cuisine create. By destroying the Holy Temple and driving the people into exile, Nebuchadnezzar, in addition to becoming a somewhat unloved character, also became, albeit by fiat, the father of chicken soup. For it was only when the Jews were in exile that they developed a unique set of gastronomic specialties. One may gladly report that Jewish cuisine has survived with far more popularity than the memory of Nebuchawhatsisname.

It is primarily those Jews who eventually made their way to central and eastern Europe who evolved the cuisine that is generally associated with

1

the Jewish kitchen. This, in a way, is unfair because those Jews who found their way to North Africa, Spain and the Moslem world also developed a cuisine of their own. The Jewish fare of the Middle-Eastern and Mediterranean did not, however, vary enough from the cuisine of the region to assume, at least metaphorically speaking, a life of its own as did the food of their European cousins. It might then be better to state that in this book we are talking about that food that developed in those areas of Europe where Yiddish became the *lingua franca* of regional Jews. This makes it clear that although the food in question is distinctly Jewish, it is neither the only Jewish food nor the food of all Jews. Gefilte fish and kreplach are as alien to Ethiopian or Libyan Jews as couscous would be to the Jews of rural Prague or Breslau.

Yiddish, it must be understood, is far more than a language: Yiddish is an entire culture. Although this culture eventually reached out to incorporate Jews in major European and American cities, it had its roots in the *shtetls*, the small rural villages inhabited almost exclusively by Jews, most of whom barely eked out a livelihood. Tucked away in Russia, Poland and the Baltic states, these people lived, for several centuries, cut off from the mainstream of society. They lived devoutly religious lives, with the study of the Bible and the Talmud a major source of spiritual and intellectual sustenance.

It is simple to now romanticize this life but it was far from idyllic. More important than romanticism, however, is the reality that from these shtetls came an enormous drive for knowledge and wisdom, a powerful humanism and an exquisite sense of the beauty of the very simplest aspects of life.

No tradition other than love of the Torah was more important to the Yiddish home or village than those that centred about the preparation and consumption of food. It is reliably reported that even shtetl Jews told jokes about Jewish food, Jewish mothers and kosher chickens.

The Yiddish kitchen was not a complex one. Because the people were primarily peasants, there was little time for fineries and frills. Thus, the food that evolved was based on what was readily available, not overly expensive and at least relatively easy to prepare. There was no need to develop a large repertoire of sauces, and fancy was something left primarily to the individual imagination. It is also important to remember that in most homes the cuisine was strictly bound by the rules of cleanliness and fitness set out by the laws of *kashrut* (the kosher laws). This did not, however, stop the evolution of a highly original and broadly variegated

2

cuisine. It also led to a cuisine that prized everything and wasted nothing. From a single chicken (probably only after it had stopped giving eggs) came soup, stock, fat for future cooking, griebens (the Jewish caviar), stuffed crepes and, with just a bit of luck, a meal of leftovers as well.

Despite hardships, Yiddish culture flourished in an atmosphere, if not always of joy, certainly of hope and optimism until 1933 and the advent of Dachau and the holocaust. It is possible that the world may never understand how, between 1933 and 1945, one madman and those who followed him (actively *or* passively) could destroy much of the best of what had taken thousands of years to develop. It is well that these people know and never forget that they did not succeed. While Yiddish as a language is now spoken primarily by those of the older generation, the culture itself has endured, and has become an integral part of the lives of many Jews living in Europe, in North and South America, and in Israel. Yiddish expressions and phrases have become integrated into many languages; the tales of Shalom Aleichem and Isaac Bashevis Singer are read in over thirty languages; and by now nearly everyone in the Western world knows what a yenta is and has tasted a bagel.

More important — as in the past it was the Yiddish language that was passed on by oral tradition, it is now the Yiddish culture that has become a part of tradition. Shalom Aleichem may never have been more true to art than when he wrote: " . . . you ask what makes us continue through the ages. It's very simple, my friend. We continue because of tradition."

Notes on Food Preparation

THERE ARE SEVERAL notes on Yiddish cookery in general and on the style of this particular book with which the reader should be familiar before venturing into the recipes.

1. In keeping with tradition, the authors firmly believe that fresh foods are nearly always superior to those that are pre-prepared or packaged. Thus, reference in a recipe to mushrooms or carrots automatically implies *fresh* mushrooms or carrots and not those that have been canned, tinned, jarred, frozen or otherwise prepared. Occasional references are made to commercially packaged foods, but this is done only when experience indicates that such usage will prove better in the cooking. The authors are not didacts, however, and well aware that not all ingredients are always

3

available in fresh form. In such cases substitutions may be made according to individual discretion.

2. Concerning herbs and spices, the one rule we never violate in our own kitchens is that black pepper is always better when freshly ground. Our general rule is that herbs should be used fresh when possible while spices are frequently better when of a high quality prepared nature. The herbs and spices used primarily in the Yiddish kitchen are not many:

Spices
cinnamon
cloves
ginger
nutmeg
white pepper
black pepper
vanilla

Herbs	
bay	garlic
basil	parsley
caraway	red pepper
cumin	green pepper
dill	celery
fennel	sesame
horseradish	tarragon
mustard	thyme

3. Weights and measurements are given in both avoirdupois (ounces and pounds) and metric (grammes and kilogrammes) systems. The following will provide a quick reference for other conversions that must be made.

Conversions — Weight
2.2 pounds = 1 kilogramme
2 pounds = 900 grammes
1 pound = 450 grammes
1 ounce = 28 grammes

4

Conversions — Length
1 inch = 2½ centimetres

Abbreviations
lb = pound
oz = ounce
" = inch
kilo = kilogramme
gr = gramme
cm = centimetre
tblspn = tablespoon
tsp = teaspoon

4. When referring to oven temperatures we are speaking, in all cases, to pre-heated ovens. All cooking times are based on food being put in ovens already at the required temperatures. Oven temperatures are as follows:

	Farenheit	Centigrade
Slow	300	150
Low	330	170
Medium	350	180
Medium Hot	375	190
Hot	400	200
Very Hot	450	235

5. Concerning specific ingredients:
   a: One assumes no possible use for the skins of onions, so all references indicate peeled onions. This is true as well for carrots which should always be scraped before using in recipes.
   b: The authors have a distinct preference for cooking in butter over margarine. Whether to maintain kashrut or simply as a matter of personal taste, one may substitute one for the other.
   c: For frying we often refer to the use of chicken fat (notes for preparation on page 27). We strongly feel that this adds a special flavour to Yiddish food but if necessary for dietary reasons one may substitute a high quality vegetable oil.

5

d: Recipes frequently call for the use of chicken or beef stock (recipes on pages 77 and 78). Although we believe the use of stocks proves better in the cooking, one may, if so moved, use prepared bouillon or bouillon cubes where desired.

e: Unless specifically noted to the contrary, all references to flour imply all-purpose flour.

f: Many cooks find that the use of fresh, home-made mayonnaise enhances their dishes. For use in either salads or in cooking, we have included a recipe (page 53). Those who use commercially prepared mayonnaise should use, whenever possible, a true egg mayonnaise.

6. We have made no effort to abide by the laws of kashrut in our recipes and have thus, at times, mixed meat and dairy products (e.g. the use of chicken fat in an otherwise dairy dish). Those who are concerned with keeping a kosher home may make simple substitutions in such cases.

APPETIZERS

The Yiddish Language and the Jewish Kitchen

THAT A UNIQUE culinary style developed and was shared by the Jews of Russia, Poland, Germany, Romania and other middle and eastern European countries was rather amazing, especially in consideration of the enormous diversity between regional and national cuisines. To explain this phenomenon one need not turn to any international conspiracies, for no one, yet alone the so-called Elders of Zion, would have gone to such trouble to propagate or justify the existence of gefilte fish or noodle kugel. Nor was it the common religious or cultural traits shared by the Jews of these nations that encouraged such a cuisine to develop. One might note that not a single passage in the Old Testament refers to the renowned *kreplach*.

The mystery is easily solved, however, when one takes even a cursory glance at the Yiddish language and its impact on European Jews and their lifestyle. Based on a combination of high German, Hebrew and Slavic, linguists still debate whether Yiddish is a full-blown language or simply a dialect. The argument is unimportant, however, for Yiddish is more than either of these: Yiddish is a way of life, a culture, and a way of perceiving the universe that, while it incorporates Judaism and its principles, is even more important in first making and later describing the lives of those people who were and are involved with it.

Yiddish, it must be understood, is a polyglot tongue, ideally suited for the catch-all rubric of Jewish lifestyles. With an enormously rich vocabulary and a grammar loose enough to allow for multiple meanings, the language is ideal for the expression of the highest philosophical or literary thoughts. Together with double and triple meanings that allude to depths of joy or despair, quiet humour and even the most pragmatic daily considerations, the language is also capable of great ribaldry. In fact, as used by savants, Yiddish is sophisticated enough to contain each of these levels within a single statement.

In Yiddish the simple may either remain simple or can become very complex. In English, for example, if one is to bargain or negotiate a purchase or a business deal, the meanings of both words and actions are clear. In Yiddish, however, when one *hondels* over the price of an item under consideration, the word is far more than a descriptor of a specific action. The attempt to lower the price that is being dickered over is only a small part of the action or meaning of the word. Equally implied are certain appeals to pity, humanitarianism, justice, the fates and honour as well as to the difficulty of life. The action implied by the word is also accompanied by a modicum of hand and body gesticulation and a certain level and tone of voice, all of which are crucial to the negotiations. The word and its doing imply as well a social ritual that is followed at varying levels depending on one's ultimate understanding of the depth implied by the word. Various moments within the *hondelling* process involve feigned moves to walk out and terminate the negotiations; insults to one's lineage or intelligence; and even appeals to Heaven are, at certain critical moments, in order.

The uninitiated view the process with a certain discomfort and even alarm. What they fail to see is that both parties involved are enjoying themselves rather thoroughly. That while bargaining or negotiating is hard work, *hondelling* is one of life's assorted pleasures. The uninformed looker-on cannot possibly realize that whether the deal is concluded with a sale is not even the issue. The social exchange, the pleasure of the gambit and the game, well played, are far more important. One can always return in a day or a week to make the purchase.

The point simply stated is that bargaining or *hondelling*, when literally translated in a dictionary, are the same. But in practice the word becomes more than a language. It is an entire way of living.

One of the remarkable aspects of Yiddish, a language full of pathos and humour, is that it seems to affect even those who have no concept of the language. Woody Allen and Mel Brooks are among a host of comedians that sprinkle their speech with Yiddishisms. And everyone laughs, even if they have not the foggiest notion of what a particular word really means. The reason here, too, is simple enough: it is not only the words but a way of saying them that fills Yiddish with humour. When Woody Allen talks about his cousin the *shnook* or Mel Brooks refers to someone as a *shlemazel*, everyone knows exactly what is being implied.

The advantage in understanding does, however, belong to those who are raised with and steeped in the language. Defining a *yenta* as a woman who complains too much is as inadequate as describing men and women as intelligent bipeds; defining *chutzpah* only as unmitigated gall is as silly as referring to sharks simply as fish with large teeth. Some words in Yiddish are distinctly untranslatable except with the use of other even more untranslatable Yiddish words. *Tsimmis*, for example, while it may also be a sweet carrot side dish (which is easy enough to translate) is also a *megillah*, a *mishmash* or a *balagan*, none of which have anything to do with carrots. But when one is told not to make such a *tsimmis* of something, he or she knows precisely what is meant. As to the various personalities implied by the terms *shnook*, *shmendrik*, *shlemiel* and *shlemazel* one can only stand in awe, for only the most apocryphal stories will suffice in giving explanation, yet alone definitions.

Another of the advantages of the language is the humour inherent within its vocabulary. Terms that may be taken quite seriously in one context have quite another meaning in other uses. A *mishugena*, literally a crazy person, can also refer to a person who has an excellent sense of humour. *Mishegas*, or insanity, is frequently a word used to refer to great fun . . . or for that matter to great confusion. Even those words that have been taken directly from other languages tend to have meaning that vary both from the parent language and from moment to moment. To imply that one is either *fablungent*, *famisht* or *fatumult* can be either a terrible insult or a light, somewhat humourous compliment. Being a *kvetch* or a *nudnick* may be positive or negative, depending on context. Of course *yentas* are always *nudnicks* and *kvetches* and that is never good.

IN NO ENDEAVOUR did Yiddish have an influence as great as in the preparation and consumption of food. There may be more joy, trauma, guilt and humour centred about the supposedly simple act of dining in Jewish homes than about any other realm. Food, the kitchen and the eating habits of Jews who spoke Yiddish were all elevated to special levels in the repertoire of human experience. The Jewish mother, kitchen and psyche are inexorably tied up with the language as is the special cuisine found in the Yiddish home.

It is in relation to food that the language may be most prone to the development of nostalgia. Jews from Yiddish backgrounds, regardless whether they are old enough to have survived the later pogroms or the holocaust or if they are the grandchildren of these people, reminisce about the old country, former neighbours, an older way of life. But mostly they remember and talk about the food. For kishke, kreplach, kugel, kneidelach, challah and tsimmis there are no substitutes.

The use of Yiddish is on the wane now. Those Jews who left Europe between the 1920's and the mid-century still use the language but their *lingua franca* has become more and more that of their adopted countries. What remains, at least in public, the most obvious leftover of Yiddish is the accent. The children and grandchildren of these refugees, while they may understand the language to varying degrees, rarely speak it. Only in the Soviet bloc where many Jews continue to reside, voluntarily or otherwise, and in several Middle-European nations does the Jewish community continue to rely heavily on Yiddish and in many places it is Hebrew that for political and social reasons is becoming a more desirable language. In Israel one hears Yiddish primarily in certain ultra-orthodox neighbourhoods or in the cafes when older people from various old countries get together.

What does and will continue, at least for a long, long while, to survive are those parts of the Yiddish culture and vocabulary that so dominate the eating habits of the people. Although the language itself may be lost in the homes of many young people, the habits and styles that the language implied are still eminently present. Chicken soup is still seen as the best cure for a nearly infinite number of medical disorders; the Yiddish mother no less today than in earlier times remains the primary source of love and *tsuris* (troubles) for her children with regard to food in general and their eating habits in particular. It may even be through the kitchen that the language will survive. Nobody will ever be foolish enough to translate *kugel mit luchsen* and the world, whatever its failings, will never be foolish enough to give up *kugel mit luchsen*.

D.R.

11

The Fabulous Gefilte and Other Stories

There are three things which are too wonderful for me, Yea, four which I know not.

Proverbs 30:18

IN THE YIDDISH kitchen one never refers to *hors d'oeuvres*. Such snobbery has no place in the *haemishe* (homelike) kitchen. An appetizer by any other name remains an appetizer and, although it may sometimes be pronounced as *eppitizer*, it is never called by an obscure French name.

The best known of Jewish appetizers is probably gefilte fish, and the fame of this delight has spread well beyond the Jewish kitchen. Canned, jarred and other commercially prepared gefilte fish has found its way into such unlikely places as Harlem grocery stores, delicatessen shops in Geneva and supermarkets on small Greek islands. Nearly everyone loves gefilte fish but not too many realize that there is no fish, at least on this planet, known as gefilte.

While Jews of various religious persuasions, ranging from the ultra-orthodox zealots of Williamsburg in Brooklyn or of Mea She'arim in Jerusalem to the most reform Jews of Connecticut or Tel Aviv, differ in their interpretations of the Creation as described in the book of Genesis, none argue with regard to the gefilte. This was one of the creatures with which the Creator did not populate the earth. It was left to a Jewish cook some many years later to make up for this oversight. Here again, though the argument begins anew (and Jews, orthodox or other, thrive on argument), because there are so many ways in which one may create a gefilte.

Whether the ideal gefilte fish (and with gefilte fish one always strives for an ideal) is composed entirely of ground carp; a mixture of carp and whitefish; or of carp, whitefish and perch, is only one bone of contention. Other urgent issues deal with the texture of the finished product (anywhere from extremely fine to somewhat coarse is acceptable); and the nature of the jellied sauce that sometimes accompanies it. The quality, colour and strength of the horseradish that is served as a condiment is also perceived as a critical factor, both in the eating and the debate.

As a result of both the popularity and the debate, most Jewish cooks have a fairly individualized recipe of their own. Most also have a memory of a particularly favourite gefilte fish. Both the memories and the recipes have frequently come from family members, and parents have been known to forever traumatize their children with debates over the superiority over Bube Gittel's or Tante Razel's gefilte fish.

One would be mistaken to think that such debates are confined to the 19th or early 20th century characters in an Isaac Bashevis Singer novel. This is not the case, for even the grand and great-grandchildren of earlier immigrants to North and South America, England or Israel carry on these debates in the spirit of devoted seekers of truth.

The debates over gefilte fish invariably trigger memories and tales, whether remembered personally or passed down over two or more generations, of various family members and their antics and traits. Of Tante Razel whose lover ran off with a movie star and took with him in the process her jewellery, fur coat and cash; of Uncle Doovid who used to come to play marbles on the carpeted floor; of Grandpa Osher and his huge roll-top desk and home-spun philosophy; of Bube Gittel who, while she may have been the world's outstanding nudnik, managed to charm her family until well over her allotted hundred years. And for all the *tsuris* (difficulties) comes the acknowledgement that it is not so bad, after all, to be a Jew. After all, if not to us, to whom else did it fall to discover the delightful gefilte?

D.G.

Gefilte Fish — 1

3 ½ lbs (1 ½ kilo) carp or pike
2 medium onions, grated finely
4 tblspns matzo meal
3 eggs
8 cups broth (page 15)
salt and pepper to taste

1. Clean, bone and skin the fish reserving head, skin and bones for broth. Grind the fish finely using either a meat grinder or food processor and add the onions, matzo meal, eggs and seasonings. To this add ¼ cup cold water and mix well. The mixture should be fluffy and a bit sticky. If too thick add small amounts of water as needed.
2. Prepare the broth (page 15).
3. Hand-shape the mixtures into balls about 2″ (5 cm) in diameter and gently place these in the simmering broth. Add water to cover if necessary, cover lightly and simmer over low flame for 1 hour.
4. Remove balls from the broth with a slotted spoon and set aside to cool. Strain the broth and pour over the fish balls. Garnish with carrots from the broth. May be served hot or cold. If served cold, set in refrigerator, covered, until the broth jells. Serve with prepared red horseradish.

Serves 6-8.

Gefilte Fish — 2

1 large carp, whole, about 3 ½ lbs (1 ½ kilo)
1 medium pike, whole, about 1 ½ lbs (¾ kilo)
8 cups broth (page 15)
1 medium onion, grated finely
2 tblspns matzo meal
1 egg
salt and pepper to taste

1. Cut the carp into 2″ (5 cm) slices, leaving the head intact. Salt lightly and refrigerate, covered, for 2-3 hours.
2. Clean, bone and skin the pike reserving the head, skin and bones for broth. Grind the fish finely using either a meat grinder or food processor and add the onion, matzo meal, eggs and seasonings. To this add enough cold water

to make the mixture fluffy and a bit sticky. Be certain to mix thoroughly. Fill the carp slices with this mixture.

3. Prepare the broth (see following).

4. Gently place the stuffed slices into the simmering broth and simmer, covered, 2 hours. Remove from flame and allow to cool in the broth 20 minutes. Remove the stuffed slices carefully from the broth and set aside. Strain the broth and pour over the fish. Garnish with carrots from the broth. May be served hot or cold. To serve cold set in refrigerator, covered, until the broth jells. Serve with prepared red horseradish.

Serves 6-8.

Broth for Gefilte Fish

head, skin and bones from carp or pike
3 medium onions, sliced
3 medium carrots, sliced
1 each parsley root and celery root, cleaned
salt and pepper to taste

1. Place all ingredients in large saucepan and add 2 quarts (8 cups) water. On a high flame bring to a boil. Lower flame, allow to simmer 20-25 minutes. Adjust seasoning.

Pickled Mackerel

1 lb (450 gr) mackerel fillets
½ cup cider vinegar
4 tblspns dried bread or matzo crumbs
4 tblspns butter
2 tblspns flour
2 bay leaves
1 egg, lightly beaten
1 tsp unflavoured gelatin
½ tsp salt
¼ tsp black pepper

1. Cut the fillets into 1″ (2½ cm) slices and rub each with salt and pepper. Refrigerate, covered, for 2-4 hours.

2. Dip both sides of each fish piece first into the flour, then into the beaten egg and then in the bread crumbs. In a skillet melt the butter and in this sauté the fish until just beginning to brown. Remove from the butter and drain on paper towelling.

3. In a saucepan bring the vinegar, ½ cup water and the bay leaves to a boil. Remove from flame and set aside to cool for 10-15 minutes before stirring in the gelatin.

4. Put the fish in a low casserole dish and over this pour the vinegar mixture. Cover well and refrigerate 2-3 days before serving. Serve cold with the jellied sauce.

Serves 4.

Sweet and Sour Pike

2¼ lbs (1 kilo) pike, whole
1¼ cup cider vinegar
¾ cup brown sugar
1 carrot, sliced thinly
1 onion, sliced
1" (2½ cm) ginger root
1 parsley root, cleaned
3 cloves garlic, chopped
2 bay leaves
4 tsp seedless raisins
½ tsp each salt and allspice
¼ tsp each pepper and ground nutmeg

1. Scale and clean the fish, discarding head and tail. Cut fish into 1½" (4 cm) thick slices and put these in a saucepan with the carrot, parsley root, salt and pepper. Barely cover with water and boil until fish is tender but still firm (about 10-12 minutes). Remove from the broth and set aside to cool for 15 minutes. Put the slices in a large mouthed jar.

2. In a saucepan combine the remaining ingredients with ½ cup water and bring to a boil, allowing to boil 1-2 minutes. Remove from flame and allow to cool 15-20 minutes and then pour over the fish in the jar. Cover tightly and refrigerate at least 24 hours before serving. Serve cold. Garnish with small whole radishes.

Serves 6.

Herring Habits

A loaf of bread, a pickled herring and thou . . .
Woody Allen

IT IS SAID that the Swedes were the first people to discover the joys of pickled herring, but that is a demonstrable untruth. The honour in fact falls to a very old and somewhat senile Jewish man in Odessa who made the discovery only after accidentally storing his herring in a vinegar barrel. Only after his granddaughter discovered his error and was preparing to throw away the spoiled fish did the old man taste what he had serendipitously created. He may not have called out "Eureka", for how many old Jewish, Russian men knew Greek, but he probably did quietly mumble *machai'a* (it's a good thing). While it is true that it then took a good deal of convincing to keep the grandchild from throwing out the old man's fish, it is no less true that the fish is now put into the barrel quite intentionally, for the result was indeed a *machai'a*.

Herring, whatever its origin, is an important staple in the Yiddish kitchen and it is probably no exaggeration to say that no one enjoys it quite as much as do the older men of any family. It is partly the herring and partly the ritual that accompanies its eating that contributes to the pleasure. And a ritual there is indeed.

Herring, while it is frequently served with breakfast or as an appetizer, is more important to the Jewish diet when taken as a *nosh* (snack) anywhere in the day from two in the afternoon until three in the morning. It may be consumed while in a restaurant, a cafe (there are many, especially in New York, London, Paris and Tel Aviv that cater to such specific appetites) or at home but the ritual is invariably the same.

The herring should always be served on a plate just a bit shorter than the length of the fish. That is to say, there should be just a bit of herring hanging over the edges. Whether this is intended as a sign of affluence or simply because most herrings are longer than most plates is unknown. Equally important is that the herring always be accompanied by a single slice of bread, two pieces of onion and a glass (but never, never a cup) of hot tea with two half cubes of sugar on the side or a glass of schnapps (with sugar optional).

The true herring *maven* (devotee) sits down to his herring with a Yiddish newspaper (although other languages will suffice), a suspicious gleam in the eye with which the plate is inspected, and a large napkin which is spread over the lap if the herring meets with visual approval. One may sit in the company of others but only if they too are devoted to their plates, for discussion during the process of dining on herring dulls the appreciative abilities of the senses. (One should not misunderstand: during most dining, discussion or even heated debate increases the appreciation of food. It is only herring that proves the exception to this rule.)

The process of eating the repast is simple enough: a delicate slice of herring, a bite of onion, a tad of bread and a sip of tea or schnapps in that order. And the repetition of that process in a leisurely fashion until the plate has been wiped clean by the last bit of bread. The appearance of leisure is important to the process. The herring eater should feel and appear to have literally all of the time in the world with which to consume his fare. A true *maven* will devote a minimum of forty minutes to the consumption of a single slice of herring. This allows adequate time for perusing the newspaper, for thoughts on a higher plane and for an evaluation of the herring at hand. Only afterwards may a second cup of tea be served and discussion ensue.

It has been said that old men find no greater *nachas* (pleasure) than that they find in their herring. That may be a bit of exaggeration. Only a bit.

D.L.

18

Salt Herring with Apples

8 salt herring fillets
1 cup sour cream
¾ cup vinegar
8 whole peppercorns
2 medium onions, sliced thinly
2 apples, peeled, cored and sliced
2 whole bay leaves
2 tblspns mayonnaise
1 tsp sugar
¾ tsp prepared mustard

1. Soak the herring fillets overnight in water, changing water several times. Drain and cut the fillets into 1″ (2½ cm) slices.
2. In a saucepan put the vinegar, bay leaves, sugar and peppercorns. Cover and boil for 5 minutes. Set aside to cool for 15 minutes. Add the sour cream, mustard and mayonnaise, mixing well.
3. In a mixing bowl mix the apples and onions and over these pour 1½ cups boiling water. Steep 10 minutes and drain.
4. In a large mouthed jar alternate layers of herring with layers of apples and onions. Pour the marinade over and close tightly. Refrigerate for 3 - 4 days before serving. Serve cold.

Serves 6 - 8.

Pickled Herring with Apples

3 fillets pickled herring
4 sour apples
3 medium onions, chopped finely
6 tblspns mayonnaise
½ cup sour cream
juice of 2 small lemons
1 tsp sugar
¼ tsp each salt and pepper

1. Peel and dice the apples and cut the herring into 1″ (2½ cm) cubes.
2. Mix well the mayonnaise, sour cream, lemon juice and seasonings. Into a

bowl put the apples, onion and herring. Add the sauce and mix well. May be served chilled or at room temperature.

Serves 3-4.

Herring in Honey

10 salt herring fillets
2 onions, sliced thinly
1 lemon, peeled and sliced thinly
½ cup seedless raisins
1½ tblspns honey
dash each cinnamon, pepper, ground ginger

1. Soak herring fillets overnight and then rinse thoroughly. Roll the fillets and fasten with wooden toothpicks. Put the rolled fillets in a wide-mouthed jar.
2. Into a saucepan with 2 cups boiling water, add the onions and raisins. Lower flame and simmer, partly covered, for 1½ hours, adding water if necessary. At the end of this time add the honey, spices and lemon and continue cooking for 15 minutes. Remove from heat and discard the lemon slices. Pour this sauce and the onions over the herrings. Allow to cool, uncovered, for 25-30 minutes and then close tightly. Refrigerate 2-3 days before serving.

Serves 5 or 10.

Herring in Sweet Cream

10 herring fillets
1 large onion, sliced thinly
½ cup heavy cream
1 tblspn each sugar and wine vinegar

1. By hand or with an electric mixer, whip the cream and sugar until stiff. Fold in the vinegar.
2. Cut each herring fillet in 3 or 4 pieces and place these with the onion slices in a wide-mouthed jar. Over these pour the cream mixture. Cover and refrigerate until well chilled. Serve cold.

Serves 5 or 10.

Matjas Herring in Sour Cream

4 Matjas herring fillets
4 large onions, halved
1 cup sour cream
⅓ cup mayonnaise
2 carrots, grated coarsely
1½ tsp vinegar
1 tsp sugar
Tabasco to taste

1. Soak the onions in cold water for from 4-6 hours. Soak the herring in cold water for ½ hour.
2. In a bowl put the mayonnaise, sour cream, vinegar and sugar. Mix well. Shred the onion thinly and place in the bowl. Add remaining ingredients and stir well with wooden spoon. Refrigerate and serve cold.

Serves 6-8.

Matjas Herring in Oil

4 Matjas herring fillets
¾ cup milk
2 medium onions, sliced
6 whole peppercorns
olive oil as needed

1. Cut the fillets into 2″ (5 cm) pieces. Cover with water and let stand 1 hour. Drain, rinse and soak in the milk 1 hour.
2. Remove the herring slices from the milk and place in 1 pint (½ litre) jar. Add peppercorns, onions and oil to cover. Close tightly and refrigerate 1 week before serving. Serve cold.

Serves 2 or 4.

Matjas Herring with Onions

1 lb (450 gr) Matjas herring, whole
2 medium onions
2½ tblspns olive oil
1 tblspn vinegar
½ tsp white pepper

1. Clean the herring, remove the bones and cut in small pieces.
2. Slice the onion and separate into rings. Combine the herring and onion rings and sprinkle over the pepper. Over this sprinkle the oil and vinegar. Garnish with small radishes and tomato wedges.

Serves 4.

You Expected Maybe Pâté de Foie Gras?

I was not at ease, neither was I quiet, neither had I rest . . .
Job 3:26

NO ONE has *tsuris* (troubles) like Jewish waiters have *tsuris. Oy*, as it might be said, have they got *tsuris.* And no one enjoys sharing those problems with others as does this very special clan. One has only to enter a Jewish restaurant to discover precisely how it all works.

Regardless of whether the eatery is Rappaport's in Paris, The Famous in Brooklyn, Ratner's in Manhattan or Batia's in Tel Aviv, the phenomenon is virtually identical. It seems inescapable that all Jewish waiters hold certain traits in common. First of all, regardless of their true age, they all try to give the appearance of very, very old men. Rather than walking in the style to which most mortals are accustomed, they seem to shuffle painfully from place to place. They also share the commonality of terribly limited peripheral vision: that is to say, Jewish waiters never see clients waving for their attention until it is convenient for them to see such waving. Third, whatever a client orders, the waiter will invariably look upon him or her with a certain amount of disdain and suggest something else. Finally, the Jewish waiter invariably walks a fine line that borders somewhere between forced politeness and outright insolence which seems directed both at the proprietor of the restaurant and its clientele.

Questions are always answered with questions. "What's good today?" is countered with "You were expecting something bad today?"; "How's the chopped liver?" is answered with "How should the chopped liver be?"; and even an attempt at mollifying the waiter with "What do you recommend?" is met with "So, what should I recommend?".

Implied in these traits are several other descriptors which apply. The waiters in these establishments always seem just a bit removed from being quite as clean as one would like; their hearing abilities always seem a bit impaired, and they always look very tired indeed. They do not so much "serve" food as they put plates on the table accompanying such action with a certain amount of rattle and other noise; they rarely bring the various courses in the order that one expects; and they take on a terribly pained look when accused (no matter how gently) of having made an error in adding up the bill.

One must acknowledge that the work of a waiter, Jewish or not, is physically demanding and difficult. Thus, a certain amount of sympathy is in order. The problem with the Jewish waiter, especially when working in a Jewish restaurant, is that he expects not sympathy but pity, and while his shenanigans do add to the charm of one's meal, pity is hard to come by.

Traditional Jewish restaurants, no less than the waiters that work in them, also have several shared traits. They are rarely luxurious in nature, the tile floors, plain furnishings and simple decor taking second place to the food and ambiance. They are frequently housed in older buildings and it is considered a positive rather than a negative attribute that the furnishings are rather old (although never antique) and worn. Rarely air-conditioned, most rely on overhead ceiling fans for a bit of coolness during the summer months. The silver is rarely polished and slightly chipped plates are the rule rather than the exception. Most boast, in lieu of a mâitre d'hôtel or a cashier who sits at a panelled desk, a cash register no less than 65 years old and a cashier at least fifteen years older than that. Some maintain the mood, if not the actuality, of sawdust on the floors and nearly all feature large plate glass windows with no trace of draperies.

My own first experience with a Jewish restaurant dates back nearly 45 years. I remember dining on chopped chicken liver, *kashe veronishkes* and *kishke*. And I seem to remember the waiter asking, just a bit cynically, "*Nu?* You expected maybe *pâté de foie gras?*" Since that time I have dined in the same Jewish restaurant and with that same waiter in at least twenty different cities in ten different countries. I am pleased to report that although I have indeed eaten and enjoyed *pâté de foie gras* it has never been in a Jewish restaurant.

D.R.

Chopped Chicken Liver — 1

1 lb (450 gr) chicken livers
4 hard boiled eggs
2 green onions, finely chopped
juice of ½ lemon
salt and pepper to taste
oil for frying

1. In a skillet heat enough oil to fry the livers. When the oil is hot add the livers and fry, turning occasionally, until done. Remove the livers from the oil and drain on paper towelling. Dice the liver finely.
2. Shell the eggs and dice finely. Add these to the liver and then add the green onion, salt, pepper and lemon. Mix well and refrigerate. Serve well chilled on lettuce leaves.

Serves 4 - 6.

Chopped Chicken Liver — 2

2 lbs (900 gr) chicken livers, halved
3 large onions, chopped
3 hard boiled eggs, chopped
4 tblspns chicken fat
1 ½ tsp salt
½ tsp black pepper

1. Under hot broiler cook the livers until well browned on both sides and lightly browned through (about 5 - 6 minutes on each side). Chop the livers finely by hand or in a food processor.

2. In a skillet melt the chicken fat and in this sauté the onions until just golden.
3. Combine all ingredients and mix thoroughly. Serve well chilled on lettuce leaves and garnished with green olives.

Serves 6-8.

Egg Salad

8 hard boiled eggs, grated coarsely
2 medium onions, chopped finely
2 tblspns oil
¼ tsp each salt and white pepper
2-3 drops Tabasco (optional)

1. Mix well all the ingredients. Refrigerate and serve well chilled. May be served on lettuce leaves and garnished with small green olives.

Serves 4-6.

Eggplant Salad

1 large eggplant
¼ cup onion, finely chopped
¼ cup green pepper, finely chopped
2 tblspns each lemon juice and mayonnaise
salt and pepper to taste

1. In a hot oven bake the eggplant until meat is tender and skin is well charred. Remove from heat, slit the eggplant in 2-3 places and let cool before peeling. With a fork mash the pulp coarsely and add the onions and green pepper. Blend in the remaining ingredients and store, covered, in refrigerator until ready for use. Serve on lettuce leaves and garnished with black olives.

Serves 4-6.

Eggs and Onions

8 hard boiled eggs
12 spring onions, chopped finely
1 large red pepper, diced coarsely
3 tblspns margarine
1 tblspn olive oil
½ tsp salt
pepper to taste

1. Mash the eggs together with the spring onion, oil, margarine and salt and pepper. To this add the diced red pepper and mix thoroughly. Refrigerate and serve chilled on lettuce leaves. Garnish with black olives.

Serves 4 - 6.

Calf's Foot Jelly

1 calf foot, cut in pieces
4 cloves garlic, crushed
2 small onions
2 carrots
2 hard boiled eggs
½ tsp each salt and pepper

1. Put the foot pieces in a saucepan and cover with water. On a high flame bring to a boil and allow to boil rapidly for 2 - 3 minutes. Discard the water and cover the foot with fresh cold water.
2. Add the onions, carrots and pinch of salt. Bring to a boil and then lower flame. Cook, covered, on lowest possible flame overnight (minimum 6 hours) until the meat separates from the bone. Remove from the flame, reserving the liquid.
3. Remove meat from bones and chop finely. Add to the meat the garlic, salt and pepper and mix well.
4. Slice the hard boiled eggs and place them in a single layer in an attractive serving casserole. Over this distribute the meat mixture and then pour over the liquid in which the foot was cooked. (The serving dish should be such that the depth of the mixture is no less than 1½″ [4 cm].) Allow to cool and

then refrigerate, covered, until the mixture jells. Cut in squares. Garnish with lemon wedges.

Serves 8.

Meat Balls in Tomato Sauce

1 lb (450 gr) ground beef
1 cup tomato sauce
2 large onions, chopped
6 oz (200 gr) tomato purée
juice of 2 lemons
1 egg
2 tblspns bread crumbs
2 tblspns brown sugar
1½ tblspns oil
½ tsp salt
¼ tsp black pepper

1. In a skillet sauté the onions in hot oil until golden brown. Transfer the onions and the oil to a large mixing bowl and add the ground beef, bread crumbs, egg, salt and pepper. Mix well and form into 1″ (2½ cm) balls.
2. In a saucepan combine the remaining ingredients and to this add the meatballs and water to just cover. Bring to a boil, cover and lower flame, allowing to simmer for 1 hour. Serve hot.

Serves 4.

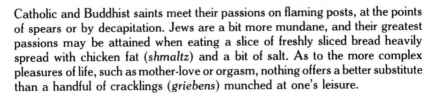

Chicken Fat and Cracklings
Shmaltz und Griebens

Catholic and Buddhist saints meet their passions on flaming posts, at the points of spears or by decapitation. Jews are a bit more mundane, and their greatest passions may be attained when eating a slice of freshly sliced bread heavily spread with chicken fat (*shmaltz*) and a bit of salt. As to the more complex pleasures of life, such as mother-love or orgasm, nothing offers a better substitute than a handful of cracklings (*griebens*) munched at one's leisure.

fat and fatty skin of 1 large chicken
salt to taste
1 large onion, chopped coarsely

1. Cut the fat and skin into small pieces, sprinkle with salt and place these in a heavy skillet. Over a low flame cook these, stirring frequently, until skin has browned. Add the onions and sauté until these are golden-brown, and the cracklings are crunchy (about 15 minutes). Remove from flame and take out the onions and cracklings with a slotted spoon. If you can refrain from eating these directly, place them in a jar, seal and refrigerate.

2. Strain and cool the fat. Store and refrigerate, covered, in a separate jar.

Breakfast at Tiffany's

We Jews are o.k. After all, who gave the world Einstein? Who gave them Freud? Who gave them bagels and lox?

Marty Feldman

WORLD CULINARY favourites have the nasty habit of being expensive. Of even modicum amounts of true Beluga caviar most ordinary mortals can only dream and the mere thought of serving even a reasonable portion of hummingbird tongues is enough to make the bank account rattle. The prices of smoked salmon and sturgeon are so high that even the proprietors of gourmet shops are embarrassed by them. It may be that the last refuge of the feast that features huge amounts of fine caviar, salmon and sturgeon is at the parties thrown by the various Soviet ambassadors when they are trying to impress their diplomatic peers with the riches of mother Russia. Even the Soviets, however, can no longer afford hummingbird tongues.

But Jews have found a solution, at least to the smoked salmon problem. Despite the outrageous price of *lox* (the "real" name of smoked salmon if one happens to be either Jewish or otherwise well informed), it is still within the realm of possibility of having friends or family dine on this true luxury for only a small outlay of one's life savings. It is simple enough — one need only put out a small amount of lox, a large helping of cream cheese and a huge pile of bagels. And let them eat sandwiches.

Surprisingly enough this is not a deception of any sort, for good lox has quite enough flavour to make itself eminently well known on a sandwich with these particular ingredients.

The first thing one must realize is that there are two varieties of lox — belly and Nova Scotia. Belly lox is somewhat saltier than the Nova Scotia variety but whether the one is "better" than the other is merely a matter of dialectics. It is true, however, that those people who have come from the old country will invariably swear that those who buy the Nova Scotia variety are simply the *nouveaux riches* showing off. All arguments aside, let it be known that either will serve admirably on a bagel sandwich.

As to bagels one should know that a bagel of quality will have a deep brown crust and should feel just the least bit doughy on the palate. The crust may or may not be slightly salted, depending on individual taste. Bagels also find themselves in two varieties — egg and water, the only difference in the making being the addition of eggs to the batter in the first case. Though the egg bagel is a bit richer, it is to the water bagel that go the honours for use together with lox.

The rules for preparing bagels and lox are simple enough. The bagel should be sliced in half along its diameter, the cream cheese should be spread generously and then the lox placed (lovingly) in position before closing the sandwich. The rules for eating are only a bit more complex. In addition to the usual signs of appreciation one always pays a host or hostess, when dining on this particular delight one should also include a modicum amount of lip smacking, a periodic patting of the tummy and an occasional "*Oy*, that's good!" (*Oy*, it should be noted, depending on how it is used can be either a positive or negative expression.)

While it is generally highly acceptable to dunk bagels into one's coffee this is a definite no-no when the bagel has been combined with cream cheese and lox. It not only spoils the lox and the coffee, it invariably devastates one's host. And at those prices such behaviour should be avoided.

D.G.

SOMEWHERE IN-BETWEEN

Sigmund Freud, the Knishe and Other Atavisms

WHEREAS IT WAS Hung Tse Wu, the great chef of the Han Dynasty, who first shared his recipes with the Chinese masses, it was the magnificent Escoffier who made the French aware of their gourmet nature. Jews, never particularly reputed as gourmet chefs but invariably known as lovers of good food, were made aware of their particular oral nature by Sigmund Freud, that not-so-humble psychoanalyst who elevated both eating habits and guilt feelings to a near art-form among his people.

Jews, it should be understood, feel guilt about nearly everything. They feel a personal sense of guilt because the Creator did not do a more perfect job in establishing this best of all possible worlds and they feel guilty because they dare to fault God for His imperfections. They feel guilty when the world persecutes them or when they are ignored. It's a heckuva bind, and not restricted to such cosmic issues alone. Even everyday life is ridden with guilt.

Such feelings are aroused for not loving one's parents enough, for loving one's children *too* much, for working too hard or not hard enough. There is guilt whether one makes love too often or not often enough and over the amounts one does or does not eat, especially when at one's parents' home. Phillip Roth's endearing character, Portnoy, was the grand-master of the guilt complex. Portnoy felt guilt over his body, his personality, his bowel movements and his choice of sexual partners. Portnoy had a problem.

Despite being a generally intelligent people there is little to alleviate the situation. Knowing that most of these feelings are unnecessary only instills a further sense of guilt over the guilt one is feeling. To make it even more complex, during the rare guilt-free moment one is overwhelmed for *not* feeling guilty.

It goes full circle. Jewish mothers who feel guilty that they are not loving enough to their children overcompensate by feeding the kids too much. The kids feel guilty because it must, after all, be their own behaviour that makes their mothers feel so badly. So to help the mothers, the kids eat. And they then feel guilty because they have become too fat from eating too much. Sooner or later these kids have children of their own and whole new cycles of guilt are generated about relationships with grandchildren. It continues . . .

Freud was quite right in indicating that people tend to sublimate or otherwise deal with their guilt. One of the methods that Jews have devised in their sublimation is through their eating habits. In the event, for example, that regular meals do not offer adequate opportunity for sublimation, Jews have invented an entire category of foods that are meant to be consumed *between* meals. If one is overwhelmed by guilt during the course of the day he or she need only run out to the nearest delicatessen and munch on an assortment of treats to fill both the stomach and the psyche. To Freud, the highest form of sublimation was in artistic creations, and it may be in no realm that Jewish food has attained as high a form as in the snack.

The *nosh* (snack) falls into two distinct categories — *delicatess* and *chuzerai*, and if one is to fully appreciate either the Yiddish language or the Jewish psyche and eating habits, these words need a bit of examination.

The first two terms are taken directly from high German. *Noshing* is a term somewhat onomatopoeic in nature that is taken from the sound of teeth when they are masticating or, if one wants to trace the word even further, gnashing. Thus, *nosh* or *nasherei* (plural form) is food on which one munches. *Delicatess* describes foods that are considered delicate to the palate, and it is from this stem that the word delicatessen is taken. *Chuzerai*, on the other hand, derives from Hebrew where a *chazir* is a pig. The pig has been traditionally viewed in Judaism as forbidden or "dirty" food, thus, in Yiddish, *chuzerai* refers to food that is somehow unacceptable. In modern jargon, *chuzerai* is junk food.

The semantics problem is simple enough but there the simplicity ends, for although every Jew above the age of six has established for him or herself the differences between what is and what is not *chuzerai*, there is no concensus beyond the level of the individual. There is no connection in this particular decision-making process with the laws of *kashrut* for what is kosher is kosher and what is not simply is not. The question is far more complex — even if something is kosher is it acceptable *nosherei* or is it simply junk? There may be no other point where individuals move further away from collective Jewish norms than in this particular realm.

For this author it may best be summed up by stating that to my personal experience there are sublime knishes on three continents, North and South America and Europe, but the best knishes by far came from Moshe Pippick's on Manhattan's lower East Side. There are superb kneidelach in at least thirty cities, but the best of the lot come from Cohen's Bakery on Rue du Chat Noir in Paris. And by far the world's best blintzes (even though one may find superb blintzes in many cities) are served at Stern's Cafe in Geneva.

Freud dined at both Cohen's and Stern's. He never sampled the fares at Mr. Pippick's. I feel absolutely no guilt over that.

D.R.

So, What's a Blintz?

How do you describe a love so great . . .
                        Erich Segal

AT LEAST SINCE the time of the Pharaohs it has been a popular (and sometimes devastating) international sport to blame nearly every catastrophe, natural or otherwise, on the Jews. While it is not particularly comforting to be a universal scapegoat, there is at least some satisfaction to be found in the knowledge that Judaism has outlived most of the empires and tyrants that have tried to destroy it. Jews have learned to cope and although such oppression may not be at all pleasant it may be understood and gone beyond. What *is* untenable, however, is the world attitude towards blintzes!

Despite the fact that Jews have been making and eating blintzes for over a thousand years, the discovery of this particular delicacy is claimed by the Hungarians, the French, the Poles, the Russians and even the usually democratic Americans. No one gives credit to the Jews.

We would do well to define the blintz in question but this raises something of a problem, for defining something unique leads to a semantic difficulty. It simply does not suffice to state the obvious: a blintz is a blintz is a blintz. It may, however, be possible to attain our definitional goal by describing the blintz by what it is *not*.

A blintz is definitely not a crepe. Despite the multiple charms of crepes (Suzettes or otherwise), no French crepe is worthy of the name of blintz. They are simply too fragile, too foppish and a bit too snobbish to do justice to the true blintz. Nor is the blintz an American flapjack or griddlecake. This is not to say that flapjacks lack their own charm but one would no sooner make a blintz that unnecessarily thick as they would destroy its flavour by annointing it with inordinate amounts of maple syrup. Nor is the blintz merely a pancake. Pancakes, at least in the Yiddish kitchen, consist primarily of potato and spice mixtures which are deep fried. As delicious as the standard pancake (or *latke*) is, it just doesn't qualify as a blintz.

The blintz is unique in several other ways as well. Unlike griddlecakes or flapjacks which are invariably perceived as fare for the breakfast table or crepes which, despite their multiple forms, are most often found served as desserts, the blintz is infinitely versatile. At times blintzes will prove eminently appropriate for breakfast; they may frequently be served for lunch; and they suffice handily for a snack. They also make for magnificent desserts. Blintzes, in a word, are better than any of their cousins.

By a joint process of elimination and deduction the astute reader has by now calculated that the blintz is considered, at least by Jews and others who claim it as their own, quite a delicacy. They have also concluded that the blintz is a pancake-like dough based mixture, fried on a griddle and then stuffed with an assortment of tasties ranging from salted or sweet cheeses to chocolate mousse or raspberry soufflé. As to the ultimate value of blintzes it should be noted that the arch anti-semites Ferdinand and Isabella of Spain employed a special chef for the preparation of their blintzes. So impressed were they with the art of their blintz-chef that he was one of the few Jews who was neither exiled, forcefully converted or burned at the stake of the Inquisition. Not a bad deal for a blintz-chef.

D.L.

Blintzes

1 cup flour
2 eggs, beaten
¾ tsp each baking powder and salt
¼ tsp sugar
butter for frying
filling of choice (see following)

1. Sift together the flour, salt and sugar. Add the baking powder and then the water. Blend thoroughly until smooth. The batter should be somewhat runny. If overly thick, add water as necessary.
2. Heat a crepe pan or medium-sized skillet over a high flame and brush with a small amount of butter. Pour in enough of the batter to barely coat the bottom of the pan and immediately tilt and shake the pan so that the batter covers the entire bottom. Cook until the batter stops bubbling and edges begin to separate from the pan. Slide the individual blintzes onto a clean towel. Do not re-grease the pan unless necessary and repeat the process until all blintzes are made.
3. In the centre of each blintz place 1 - 1½ tblspns of the selected filling and roll up the blintzes, folding sides over to seal.
4. In a large skillet melt 3 tblspns butter and in this fry several blintzes at a time, until golden brown on both sides. Serve hot, garnish with sour cream, confectioners' sugar or a mixture of confectioners' sugar and cinnamon.

Yields 10 - 12 blintzes.

Fillings for Blintzes

Cheese — 1

½ cup each cottage cheese and softened cream cheese
1 egg, beaten
2 tsp sugar
¼ tsp each salt and nutmeg

1. Mix all ingredients together thoroughly.

Cheese — 2

¾ lb (350 gr) Emmenthal or similar cheese, grated
⅓ cup cottage cheese
2 tblspns sugar
1 egg, beaten

1. Mix all ingredients together thoroughly.

Cheese — 3

1½ cups cottage cheese
2 egg yolks, beaten
1 tsp butter, softened
1 tsp grated lemon rind

1. Mix all ingredients together thoroughly.

Liver

1 lb (450 gr) chicken livers
2 hard boiled eggs
1 large onion, chopped coarsely
½ tsp salt
pepper to taste
oil for frying

1. In a skillet heat a small amount of oil and in this sauté the chicken livers and onions until nicely browned. In a blender or food processor, together with the oil, hard boiled eggs, salt and pepper, purée until the mixture is smooth.

Apple

3 large cooking apples, peeled, cored and grated finely
½ cup seedless raisins or ground almonds
1 egg, well beaten
1½ tblspns dried bread crumbs
1 tblspn sugar
½ tsp cinnamon
¼ tsp each ground cloves and nutmeg

1. Mix all ingredients together thoroughly.

A Bias for Brooklyn

GEFILTE FISH, properly made, has often been described as delectable; herring of the best varieties is mild; chopped liver at its best is smooth; and good blintzes are said to have an air of delicacy. For the knishe no such terms apply. There is absolutely no gentilesse to the knishe which, with no subtlety whatever slams into the palate and, when swallowed, drops rather heavily from gullet to stomach.

One simply cannot be unaware of a knishe. The flavour is powerful and even the scent is strong enough to linger for more than a few moments. Because they are unimaginably dense, it takes a certain effort to chew them and the digestion process is not a simple one.

To the uninitiated it may sound quite a mystery as to why this particular dish remains a favourite among Jewish snack foods. Those in the know recognize that it is precisely these odd qualities that make the knishe a highly desirable treat. The experienced realize that it is not only the highly spiced flavour that is so attractive; it is also the challenge in eating the knishe that is important.

Knishes, whether of the potato or kashe varieties, come in two basic sizes — small and huge. There are those just a bit larger than bite-sized which lack only the bulk that some devotees admire. And there are the larger ones. A survey of dedicated knishe fans indicates that the ideal knishe measures some five inches (thirteen cm) square and about one inch (two and a half cm) thick. All agree that the outer crust should be just short of crisp and the filling a bit on the mushy side. But there agreement ends, and knishe lovers have come close to physical violence in their defence of how much salt or pepper should be placed in the batter and of precisely with what to season the finished product.

New York City's Jewish population will suffice as examples. In Brooklyn it is considered *de rigueur* to spread one side of the knishe rather heavily with special delicatessen mustard and then to eat the knishe while holding it in the hand using nothing more than a small napkin to protect one's clothing from possible ruination. Manhattanites scorn this practice and prefer only heavy salt on one side and feel secure in their belief that knishes are properly eaten with knife and fork. Bronxites have been known to use horseradish or barbeque sauce as condiments and Queens County residents are ecclectic, and thus willing to use any of these, even in some fairly odd combinations. Staten Islanders have no problem at all as Staten Island knishes are not worth eating under any circumstances.

It may be its very lack of sophistication that gives the knishe its greatest charm. Paul Bocuse, the master French chef, when introduced to the knishe, turned it over, weighing it in his hand, studied it carefully for a minute, put his nose close to it and inhaled deeply. He then put it to his mouth, took a gentle bite and tasted: And then he commented: "It's marvellous. Tell me, though, is it to be eaten or thrown at an enemy?" As a one-time Brooklynite I will vouch for its edibility — especially with a good helping of mustard on the top.

D.L.

Knishes

The Dough

2 cups flour
2 eggs, well beaten
2 egg yolks mixed with 2 tblspns water
1 tblspn oil
¾ tsp salt
1 tsp baking powder
kashe or potato stuffing (below)

1. Sift together the flour, salt and baking powder. In the centre make a well and add the oil, whole eggs and 2 tblspns water. Beat until smooth. On a lightly floured board roll out the dough to ⅛″ (¼ cm) thickness and cut into 6″ (15 cm) squares.
2. Place 2 tblspns of the filling on each square. Moisten the edges slightly, fold over and press closed. Brush tops with the egg yolk and water mixture and place on a well greased cookie tin. Bake in medium oven until golden brown (about 25-30 minutes).

Yields about 15 knishes.

Kashe Filling

1¼ cup kashe (buckwheat groats)
2 medium onions, chopped coarsely
3 tblspns chicken fat
1 egg, beaten lightly
salt and pepper to taste

1. Mix the egg and kashe well, ensuring that each grain is coated. Place the mixture in a greased baking pan and roast in a hot oven until dry (about 10 minutes). Transfer to a saucepan, pour over 1 cup boiling water and simmer on medium-low flame for 15 minutes, or until liquid is absorbed.
2. Heat the fat in a skillet and sauté the onions until golden brown. Add the onions and oil to the kashe, add salt and pepper to taste. Mix thoroughly.

41

Potato Filling

4 large potatoes, peeled and quartered
2 large onions, chopped coarsely
2 cloves garlic, finely chopped (optional)
salt and pepper to taste
3 tblspns chicken fat

1. In a saucepan cover the potatoes with lightly salted water and cook until very soft. Mash the potatoes thoroughly.
2. In a skillet melt the chicken fat and in this sauté the onions and garlic until golden brown. Combine with the potatoes and mix well. Season with salt and pepper and again mix thoroughly.

Pirogen

The Dough

1 cup flour
½ cup mashed potatoes
½ cup vegetable shortening
1 egg, well beaten
½ tsp each salt and pepper
filling (see following)
oil for frying

1. Sift together the flour, salt and pepper and mix in the mashed potatoes. After mixing well add the shortening and mix until dough is flaky. Make a well in the centre and work in the egg. Knead until the dough is smooth and elastic, adding more flour if necessary. Form the dough into a ball and roll out to ¼" (½ cm) thickness. Cut these into 3" (8 cm) rounds.
2. In the centre of each round place 1 tblspn of the filling. Stretch the dough to cover and pinch the edges together to seal forming a half-circle.
3. In a large saucepan with salted boiling water place the pirogen carefully. Allow to boil 5 minutes and remove with slotted spoon. Drain on towelling.
4. In a large skillet with hot oil at least ¼" (½ cm) deep, fry the pirogen on both sides until golden brown. Serve hot.

Yields 15 - 20 pieces.

Fillings for Pirogen

Chicken Filling

1 cup ground chicken
1 cup chicken or beef stock (pages 77-78)
1/3 cup dried bread crumbs
1 egg, lightly beaten
1 egg white, beaten stiff
1 small onion, chopped coarsely
1/4 tsp each pepper and rosemary
salt to taste
chicken fat for frying

1. Into a small mixing bowl place the stock and in this soak the bread crumbs for 2-3 minutes. Using a slotted spoon remove the bread crumbs and let drain.
2. In a skillet heat the chicken fat and in this sauté the onions and bread crumbs until onions are golden but not crisp. Mix in the ground chicken and cook 5 minutes, stirring. Stir in the whole beaten egg and the egg white. Add seasonings and mix well.

Cheese Filling — 1

1 cup cottage cheese
1/2 onion, chopped finely
1/3 cup dried bread crumbs
salt and pepper to taste
butter for frying

1. In a skillet, heat the butter and in this sauté the onion until tender. Season the cheese with salt and pepper. Add the onions and enough bread crumbs to form a firm mixture.

Cheese Filling — 2

1 lb (450 gr) farmers cheese
2 eggs, separated
3 tblspns brown sugar
1 ½ tblspns honey
1 tblspn bread crumbs
¼ tsp salt

1. Blend the egg yolks and cheese. Add sugar, honey, bread crumbs and salt. Mix well.
2. Beat the egg whites stiff and fold these into the cheese mixture.

Meat Filling

1 lb (450 gr) ground beef
2 medium onions, chopped finely
2 cloves garlic, chopped finely
1 egg, well beaten
½ tsp each salt and pepper
¼ tsp each oregano and sweet paprika
2 tblspns oil

1. In a large skillet heat the oil and sauté the onions and garlic until golden brown. Add the ground beef and seasonings and continue sautéeing until meat is browned. Add the egg, mixing well and continue cooking, stirring constantly, 2-3 minutes.

Potato Filling

2 cups mashed potatoes
2 large onions, chopped finely
1 egg, beaten
6 tblspns chicken fat
salt and pepper to taste

1. In a skillet melt 2 tblspns of the chicken fat and in this sauté the onions until golden brown. Remove from heat and add remaining ingredients, mixing well.

Potato Latkes

A Chanukkah specialty, these fried pancakes prove popular nearly any time of the year. Served with sour cream, applesauce or sugar for sprinkling over, these will generally be eaten in large quantities by family and guests. Best to prepare in large batches.

12 large potatoes, grated
3 medium onions, grated
4 eggs, beaten lightly
5 tblspns flour
3 tsp salt
1 tsp pepper
oil for deep frying

1. Squeeze out the liquid from the potatoes between towelling. (The more liquid that can be squeezed out, the better will be the latkes.) Also squeeze out the liquid from the onions. Combine all ingredients and mix together well.

2. In a heavy skillet heat oil a minimum of ¾" (2 cm) deep. When thoroughly hot drop in large spoonfuls of the batter. Latkes should be thoroughly browned and crisp on the edges on both sides. Remove with a slotted spoon and drain on paper towelling. Serve immediately or keep warm in very low oven. Serve with sour cream, applesauce or sugar for sprinkling over.

Serves 4-6, depending on how well the latkes are made.

Matzo Pancakes

1 cup matzo meal
1½ cups each water and milk
3 eggs, separated
2½ tblspns sugar
1 tsp salt
oil for frying

1. In a mixing bowl combine the matzo meal, sugar and salt. Add the water and milk, stirring well. Add the egg yolks, beating and mixing well. Set aside, covered, for 15 minutes.

2. Beat the egg whites stiff and gently fold into the matzo mixture.
3. In a large skillet heat a ½" (1 cm) layer of oil and drop into the hot oil single tablespoonfuls of the batter. Brown well on both sides and remove with slotted spoon to paper towelling. Serve immediately or keep warm in lowest possible oven. Serve with jam, sour cream, or applesauce.

Yields 12 pancakes.

Buckwheat Pancakes

2 cups buckwheat flour
3 cups buttermilk, at room temperature
½ cup flour
2 eggs, beaten
½ tsp each salt and sugar
1 tsp baking powder
butter for frying

1. Sift together all of the dry ingredients. Mix with milk and eggs until batter is smooth. Cover and let stand ½ hour.
2. Heat a crepe pan or medium-sized skillet and brush with a small amount of butter. Pour in enough of the batter to just coat the bottom of the pan and tilt and shake the pan immediately so that batter covers entire bottom. Cook pancakes on both sides until golden brown. Grease pan with butter for each pancake and repeat until batter is used. Serve hot with sour cream, jam, honey or maple syrup.

Yields about 15 pancakes.

PICKLES, RELISHES AND SAUCES

A Nickel a Pickle

Say not thou: "How was it that the former days were better than these?"
Ecclesiastes 7:10

IT MAY BE THAT Yiddish culture found its finest moment not in central and eastern Europe where it was born, but on the streets of New York City's lower East Side. The first massive wave of Jewish immigrants to that area came between 1895 and 1905 with the massive input of Russian and Polish Jews who had escaped either from the pogroms or from conscription into the Tsar's armies. This was an unmoneyed immigration consisting of peasants, intellectuals, craftspeople and merchants, and it was to streets named Hester, Orchard, Delancey and Essex that they came. The *lingua franca* was Yiddish although German, Russian, Polish and even a smattering of Hebrew and English were to be heard. All of the languages were spoken with Yiddish accents. They were orthodox and atheists, but they were Jews and they were together.

A second wave followed in the 1930s, those years just preceding the Second World War. There was even a trickle of people who came *during* the war. Those were the few who had somehow escaped the horrors of what Europe was experiencing. And this group too turned to the East

Side, especially on Saturdays and Sundays when, rain or shine, people would parade up and down on Essex Street hoping to find someone they might recognize from the old country. One might find a brother or an aunt or a *lantzman* (an emotionally laden word to which one does terrible injustice by translating only literally as "countryman"). Often the new-comers came with little money, no place to live and limited opportunities for finding work. It was on these strolls that dreams sometimes turned into realities, for a *lantzman* was somebody to be helped.

The character of the area was distinctly Jewish. It was here that Isaac Gellis established the factory which produced, in four storeys of a con-verted tenement building, the very finest kosher delicatessen. Downstairs his wife managed the small restaurant that boasted these items as specialties. A block away from Gellis' were the offices of the *New York Daily Forwards*. Known by most simply as The Forwards, this was more than just a newspaper that happened to be printed in Yiddish. It was as well a fine literary magazine and it was to its offices that Isaac Bashevis Singer and other superb Yiddish writers turned. There were a hundred bake-shops, all of which served the finest pastries. And there were dozens of cafeterias, each of which had its unique clientele. There were cafeterias for the intellectuals, for the journalists, for the artists, for the craftspeople and for the merchants. Regardless of their clientele, each specialized in *haemishe* food and in providing a comfortable place in which to sit, talk for hours and simply relax, all for the price of a cup of tea.

One of the highlights was the multitude of shops and pushcarts. What could not be bought from a pushcart on Orchard or Hester Streets probably could not be bought anywhere in America. One could find, new or used, items ranging from cups and saucers to bridal outfits to four-piece bedroom suites. And everything was negotiable. It was as if the casbah of the East and the market of the West had met in a glorious pandemonium.

Fruit stands stood side by side with tuxedos; the pickle vendor with his huge barrels on wheels would peddle his delicious sour and dill wares as he roved; and butcher shops traded next to boutiques that specialized in hand-tatted lace.

It was always crowded and hectic but it was also comfortable and somehow, despite the crowds, peaceful. It gave an aura of belonging, of being in the right place in its moment of time. There was always a valid reason for leaving the shop to sit at Rattner's and sip a glass of tea or to wander off to Moshe Pippick's for a knishe. There was time to talk with friends and it was comfortable enough that one's clients and competitors were also one's friends. It was a time when contracts were handshakes. It was a time of hope that there really would be a better day.

The mood changed sometime in 1945 when, with an incomprehensible enormity, the full weight of what had happened to six million Jews in Europe came to bear on the world. It was a time that stunned the soul. Nothing could be the same again.

THE EAST SIDE of New York retains its Jewish character even today. Although most of the push carts are gone and the common language is now English, there remain strong traces of Yiddish accents, of Jewish foods and of Jewish merchants. In Tennyson's words (although taken from a very different situation): "though much is taken, much abides." Sunday mornings are now best for the East Side. The cafeterias are open and one may still drink tea from a glass with a cube of sugar tucked into the cheek. The Jewish delicatessens still serve up their treats and there is no better cholent or salami to be found anywhere in the world. People still walk the streets looking for acquaintances. Many are older now and walk alone. And many walk primarily with their memories.

D.R.

Dill Pickles

2 lbs (900 gr) small cucumbers
4 cloves garlic
1 tblspn each salt and sugar
1 bay leaf
1 small bunch dill
½ cup white vinegar

1. Sterilize a large-mouthed one quart (1 litre) jar. Wash the cucumbers and place in the jar. Add garlic, bay leaf, sugar, salt and vinegar. Fill the jar to the brim with boiling water. Add the dill on top of the liquid. Seal tightly.
2. Allow to stand exposed to light for 7 days before serving. After opening, pickles should be refrigerated.

Pickled Carrots

16-20 medium carrots
12 peppercorns
4 whole cloves
1 cup each vinegar, sugar, water
2 tblspns mustard seeds
1 stick cinnamon

1. Clean carrots thoroughly. Cut in slices or sticks about ¼″ (½ cm) thick. Cook in lightly salted water until just tender. Remove from water and place in low baking dish.
2. Combine and mix well the remaining ingredients. Over a medium flame bring to a boil. Immediately reduce the flame and simmer, covered, 20 minutes. Pour the sauce over the carrots. Cover and refrigerate 18-24 hours. Serve cold. May garnish with chopped parsley.

Pickled Beets

4 medium beets
½ cup olive oil
6 tblspns vinegar
3 tblspns lemon juice
2 garlic cloves, finely chopped
2 tblspns each lemon juice and onion, chopped
2 tsp salt
1 tsp sugar

1. In a large saucepan place the beets and cover with lightly salted water. Cook on medium flame for about 30-40 minutes until beets are tender. Drain the beets and, under running water, remove the skins. Cut beets in thin slices. Place the slices in a wide-mouthed jar.
2. Mix remaining ingredients well and pour over the beets. Cover tightly and refrigerate 16-24 hours, turning occasionally to be sure marinade is equally distributed. Serve cold.

Horseradish Sauce — 1

½ lb (225 gr) horseradish, grated
½ cup each water and vinegar
1½ tsp sugar
1 tsp salt

1. Mix together the ingredients and adjust seasonings as necessary. May be stored if covered and refrigerated.

Yields 1 cup.

Horseradish Sauce — 2

3 tblspns horseradish, grated finely
1 cup Bechamel sauce (following)
1 tblspn light cream
½ tsp lemon juice
½ tsp each salt and pepper
Tabasco to taste

1. Combine the ingredients in a saucepan. Heat through but do not boil. Refrigerate and serve chilled.

Yields about 1½ cups.

Bechamel Sauce

1½ cups milk
1 onion, quartered
1 celery stalk, chopped
1 carrot, chopped
8 whole peppercorns
1 bay leaf
2 whole cloves
3 tblspns butter
2 tblspns flour
½ tsp salt

1. Into the top of a double boiler put the milk, onion, celery, carrot, peppercorns, bay leaves and cloves. Fill the lower section of the double boiler with water. Cover the milk mixture and heat in double boiler over low flame for about 30 minutes.
2. Strain the milk and discard the vegetables and spices.
3. Melt the butter in a skillet. Add the flour and stir continuously over low flame until an even mixture is produced. To this slowly add the milk while stirring constantly over low flame. Bring just to a boil and immediately lower flame and cook for 2 minutes. Add the salt. Keep the sauce warm until ready to serve.

Yields about 1½ cups.

Mayonnaise

Freshly made mayonnaise adds a special touch either to salads or cooking. One may, at individual discretion, substitute a commercially prepared mayonnaise. Up to the individual chef.

1 cup olive oil
2 tblspns lemon juice
2 tblspns vinegar
2 egg yolks
½ tsp each dry mustard, confectioners' sugar and salt
pinch cayenne pepper

1. Before starting be certain that all ingredients, utensils and bowls are at room temperature — about 68°F or 20°C.
2. In a mixing bowl beat the egg yolks either by hand with a wire whisk or with an electric mixer at medium speed until a uniform lemon colour is attained. To these beat in the cayenne, mustard and salt. Adding ½ tsp at a time, beat in slowly ½ cup olive oil.
3. In a separate container, combine 1½ tsp vinegar and the lemon juice.
4. To the egg yolk mixture add, alternatively, drop by drop, the vinegar-lemon juice mixture and the remaining olive oil. Stirring should be constant and the mixture should be completely smooth at the end of this process. If the mixture breaks (curdles) it may be reconstituted by placing another egg yolk in a bowl and stirring constantly while slowly adding the curdled mayonnaise.

Yields about 1½ cups.

SOUPS

Eat, My Child, It's Good For You

What is sweeter than honey? And what is stronger than a lion?
Judges 14:18

THROUGHOUT HISTORY there has been no greater fount of human nurturance, sacrifice, selflessness and devotion than the Jewish mother. Nor has any group contributed more to the anxiety levels, guilt feelings, impotence and general psychic malaise of their offspring. To add to this, no collection of people anywhere or at any time has provided the world with a greater source of humour.

Not all women who are Jewish and who happen to be mothers qualify, *ipso facto*, as Jewish Mothers. The question is not one of liberation from social norms or of profession or training. It is one of avocation, and the test is invariably in the kitchen, for it is here that Jewish motherhood takes on its most positive, negative and humourous aspects.

All Jewish mothers share certain traits in common with regard to the preparation, serving and consumption of food. The first of these is involved with making the entire family consciously aware that the food under preparation is being prepared specifically by her for them. Closely aligned with this is the notion that must be conveyed that she is doing this

56

out of love despite (emphasis on the "despite") that it is terribly difficult work. This is a subtle task for, according to the two-thousand-year-old rules of the game, nowhere during the preparation phase of the food may it be specifically stated that difficulties exist. It is only implications via passing sighs or gestures that are allowed. Sore feet, aching muscles or headaches (real or other) may never be proclaimed aloud at this point in time. In fact they must be strenuously denied, even while soaking the feet in epsom salts or when taking aspirin. Of course such suffering cannot, if it is to have its effect, go completely unseen. If, for example, no one chances to witness the aspirin-taking ritual, a bit of mild choking is appropriate. ("No, no . . . it's nothing. One of my pills just went down the wrong way.")

Offers on the part of family members to help in the preparation of food must be met with refusal. ("It's not really so difficult, I always perspire like this" or "Don't worry so, it's only a mild migraine this time.") Whether in all of this the Jewish mother is trying to establish her domain, instill a sense of appreciation or give birth to guilt complexes in her offspring is unknown, partially because so many of the psychologists who normally investigate such phenomena are Jewish and just a bit too involved with both their guilt and their mothers to be quite objective.

The serving of food is no less complex. It is critical to Jewish mother-hood that ideal timing be ensured in the preparation of the meal. That is to say, it must be a physical impossibility to serve an entire dinner at one time. Throughout dinner it is she who must constantly interrupt her own eating to lower a flame, to serve another portion or to check the oven. Jewish mothers do not eat sitting down like most family members. They spend one quarter of their time at the table and the rest running back and forth to stove, cupboard and refrigerator bringing things *to* the table. She has also timed things so that it becomes apparent that there is far too much to eat only after everyone has already eaten nearly as much as is possible. There is simply no way to consume everything that she has put out.

It is now that Mama's choicest comments are indeed in order. Those who have not devoured the overabundance that has been served up are faced with: "You don't like the way I cook anymore?" or "After all the work I did, you don't even have the courtesy to eat it?" It proves quite a catch, however, for those who do manage to eat most of the fare are then faced with: "You really think you should eat so much? You're not fat enough already?" or "Tell me, do you ever think of anything other than food?" There are no appropriate answers to such questions.

In addition to such asides, it is during the serving and consumption of the meal that discussion is invariably in order and much of the talk centres about the food that is being eaten. Here, too, every comment has its counter. "You really shouldn't have prepared so much food" is met with "It's okay. Why should it upset *me* if you don't recognize good food when you see it." "Mother, there's plenty on the table, so why don't *you* sit down and eat?" is countered by "So tell me, if *I* don't worry about you, who will?" Such maternal rebuttals never carry direct sarcasm but they do manage to convey an enormous burden of personal suffering.

Such psychological force feeding takes its toll, but one day the kids grow up and leave to establish homes of their own. One might think they have escaped but this is not true, for whether it is twice a week or once a month, they return to visit, and that invariably means they return to eat. No matter how much protestation takes place in arranging such visits ("No mother, just coffee and cake will be fine") there is invariably a full meal waiting when the kids arrive. What is odd is that the children, now adults themselves, even if they have just finished a large meal, will sit down like good boys and girls and eat. And the game starts anew. Mama serves, the kids eat; mama suffers just a little, and the kids feel just a modicum of revisited guilt.

There are, however, two interesting advantages to having grown up. By now a certain nostalgia has taken over and there is probably no memory sweeter than of those "wonderful meals my mother prepared". The other is that by adulthood the guilt patterns and ambivalent feeling towards mother and food have either been firmly established (and nothing can really be done about them short of long-term psychoanalysis) or have been well resolved (in which case nothing need be done). At any rate one is about as adjusted or as neurotic as he or she will ever be and the whole thing settles into the comfortable framework of a combination of good humour and love. And by now most of us are playing the same games with *our* children. The cycle continues . . .

D.R.

Jewish Penicillin

Whosoever shall not fall by the sword or by famine, shall fall by pestilence, so why bother shaving?

Woody Allen

MEDICAL PRACTITIONERS have speculated that insulin, sulfa and antibiotics have been the three most influential factors in extending human life. In making such an observation the medical profession demonstrates its short-sightedness, for nothing is more evident than that the single most important factor in both saving and improving the quality of life is chicken soup.

Few will question the validity of visiting a doctor when necessary or of taking the drugs they prescribe when indicated, but both doctors and most medications are relatively new to the world scene. The three drugs in question are less than a century old and medicine itself is a relatively new profession, dating back only to 420 B.C.E. when Hippocrates was a young man. Chicken soup has been around for as long as both Jews and chickens have cohabited on the planet. And that makes Hippocrates, at least on a relative time scale, an adolescent at best.

In addition to having had a long period of testing, chicken soup offers several other major advantages over most drugs. The sulfas and the antibiotics are used primarily in the treatment of various infections and insulin is taken primarily by those with certain forms of diabetes. Chicken soup, on the other hand, is good for nearly everything. As any Jewish mother, grandmother or aunt (maiden or not) can testify, a bowl of chicken soup may be used in the treatment of menstrual disorders, anxiety attacks, loneliness, arthritis, low back pain and stomach cramps. It is appropriate in cases of temporary sadness, long-term depression or ingrown toenails. It is useful not only as a cure, but as a preventive for nearly all ailments. About the only thing that no one has ever claimed for chicken soup is that it has any powers as an aphrodisiac.

What continues to amaze medical people is that chicken soup proves equally efficacious in men and women of any age or for children of either sex. It is effective whether one is Jewish or not, tastes considerably better than most of the prepared medicines that one is, from time to time, forced to take and is painless to administer (never by injection). There are no medical side effects and this delectable potion is completely non-addictive.

Whether served up for medicinal or culinary pleasure, there are several rules that one should attempt to follow in its consumption. It should always be served hot, and although it is both possible and even acceptable to eat chicken soup quietly, it is both tastier and more effective when just a bit of noise is generated between lips and spoon. The noise should never be so loud that it annoys one's table companions — a quiet *shlurping* (Yiddish and onomatopoeic but otherwise untranslatable) will suffice. The trick is in the pleasure.

D.L.

Chicken Soup — 1

1 large stewing chicken, about 5 lbs (2½ kilo) with heart, neck and gizzard
2 stalks celery with leaves, chopped coarsely
4 medium onions, whole
1 large carrot, sliced
1 parsley root, peeled and chopped
1 bay leaf
8 whole peppercorns
1½ tsp salt
pepper to taste

1. Remove skin and excess fat from chicken (reserve for use in making schmaltz and griebens). Rinse the chicken and cut into convenient pieces.

2. Place the chicken and parts in a large kettle and cover with 3 quarts (3 litres) cold water. Cover and bring to a fast boil and continue boiling 20 minutes. Uncover and skim the foam from the surface. Reduce the heat, recover and simmer 15 minutes.

3. Add remaining ingredients and continue simmering, covered, for 2 hours. Remove chicken and strain the soup. Correct the seasonings. Serve with kneidelach (page 64) or kreplach (page 64). Serve the whole onions in a separate plate. Garnish, if desired, with fresh chopped parsley.

Serves 12-16. (May be stored if refrigerated)

Chicken Soup — 2

2 lbs (900 gr) chicken wings, necks and giblets (except livers)
1½ lbs (675 gr) beef marrow or shin bones
1 large onion
4 stalks celery
1 parsnip
8 sprigs parsley
1 tblspn salt
½ tsp pepper

1. In a large kettle place all of the ingredients with 10 cups cold water. Over a high flame bring to a boil and allow to boil rapidly 2-3 minutes. Lower flame, skim off foam and cover. Let simmer gently for 2 hours.

2. Remove meat, bones and vegetables and taste. Adjust seasoning if necessary. Pour the broth through a fine sieve and serve hot. May be served *au naturel* or with kreplach, kneidelach or croutons.

Serves 6.

The Jewish Big Bang Theory

And the Lord opened the mouth of the ass, and she said . . .
Numbers 22:28

JEWISH SAGES have, for four thousand years at least, had two theories concerning the creation of the universe. The first concurs, more or less, with the Book of Genesis: that is to say, "In the beginning God created the heaven and the earth." The second, a bit more complex in nature, is frequently referred to as The Big Bang Theory. (Until 1920 this was sometimes called the Great Kvetch Hypothesis, but with the advent of quantum theory the name was judiciously changed.) According to this notion, there was a moment in time when the matter in the universe had contracted until it became so dense that it could be compressed no further. At this moment, vast energy forces in the matter took over and produced an explosion, the literally big bang, and it was this that started the complex processes of creating the universe as we now know it.

The question of real interest to Jewish physicists, mathematicians, philosophers and other metaphysicians deals not so much with what

62

happened after the big bang but what took place just before the event. Of precisely what that terribly dense material was composed is of enormous interest to Jewish scholars.

The answer is simple enough. What existed at the instant just prior to the creation was a matzo ball.

There is certain evidence to support such a notion. It is generally accepted that the material in question had to be enormously dense, and it is well known that the most dense material in the universe is a matzo ball (*kneidelach* in Yiddish). Matzo balls contain more mass in their restricted volume than any other material. As evidence of the power this creates, one may take the case of Mrs. Rozele Schwartz who resides on the 28th floor of a New York City cooperative apartment building. On March 14, 1973, Mrs. Schwartz was preparing matzo balls for chicken soup when one chanced to roll off the counter. It accelerated until it hit the floor and then went straight through, not only through each of the twenty-seven floors beneath but down to the very core of the earth. Whether this was the same matzo ball that seven seconds afterwards shot out of the earth's crust in Outer Mongolia and later went into orbit about the planet Pluto has not been confirmed but it seems a good chance.

There is another proof as well. Anyone who has ever taken too large a bite of a matzo ball can verify that when it actually hits the stomach it produces a feeling quite like that one expects of a gastro-intestinal atomic explosion. Such findings cannot be accidental nor can it be only coincidence that since 1945 kneidelach has been referred to as the Jewish Atomic Bomb.

For many of the wise men and women of Judaism, the problem was not so much in solving the creation riddle but of harnessing the energy of the matzo ball. These ancients were clearly successful, for despite the popularity of kneidelach, especially in chicken soup and with stews, there has not been a major matzo ball incident in many years. It is safe to conclude that so long as one does not live below the 28th floor of a particular cooperative apartment in New York that they will be safe if they avoid using their matzo balls either as hockey pucks or as spare wheels for their roller skates.

D.L.

Kneidelach

Like its cousin, the kreplach, this matzo dumpling goes well with chicken or other plain soups. Kneidelach may also double as dumplings with meat dishes served with gravies.

1 lb (450 gr) matzo
2 cups chicken broth
3 cloves garlic, chopped very finely
1½ tsp fresh parsley, chopped very finely
3 eggs, well beaten
1 tsp salt
½ tsp pepper (or more to taste)

1. Break the matzo into small pieces and place these in a mixing bowl. Pour over the chicken broth and steep 5 minutes. Drain the matzo and squeeze out the liquid carefully (the less liquid that remains, the better the results). Add to the drained matzo the remaining ingredients and mix well.
2. Fill a large saucepan with lightly salted water and bring to a boil. In this test the dough by dropping a small ball into the boiling water. If the dough falls apart add a small amount of matzo meal to the batter.
3. Form the batter into balls about 1″ (2½ cm) in diameter and drop these gently into the boiling water. When the matzo balls rise to the surface reduce the heat, cover and simmer gently for 15 minutes. Remove with slotted spoon.

Yields 12-15 kneidelach.

Kreplach

The Dough

1½ cups flour
2 eggs, well beaten
¼ tsp salt
filling (below)

1. Combine the ingredients with ¼ cup water and knead into a soft, sticky

dough. Roll out the dough thinly on a floured board and cut into 2" (5 cm) squares.

2. In the centre of each square place 1 tsp of filling. Fold the dough diagonally to form triangles, and press the edges closed. Take the ends of the triangle in the fingers and pinch together.

3. In a large saucepan with boiling salted water place the kreplachs. Cover and cook 20 minutes.

Chicken, Liver or Meat Filling

1 cup cooked chicken, beef liver or beef, ground
1 medium onion, chopped finely
1 egg, well beaten
2 tblspns chicken fat
salt and pepper to taste

1. In a skillet heat the chicken fat and in this sauté the onions until golden brown. Add remaining ingredients and continue to sauté 3-4 minutes.

Plain and Fancy

All ye who are hungry, come and eat.
The Passover Haggadah

THERE MAY BE NO tradition more strongly entrenched in Jewish life than that of extending the hospitality of one's home and kitchen. To some scholars the custom traces to Abraham, who opened his tent to all in the hope that they would be brought closer to God. Others feel that the tradition developed because Jews feel that any visitor may be the Messiah in disguise and that turning him away would be a sin too great to bear.

As it has come to exist today, it is considered a *mitzvah* (literally a divine commandment but in practice to most, a good deed) to feed the hungry or the stranger. In Europe, at least until half a century ago, it was traditional, for example, to invite the generally impoverished Yeshiva students to dine in different homes on each night of the week. Travellers who had to spend the Sabbath away from their own homes could count on being invited to take part in the sumptuous meal set for that day. Even passing strangers, regardless of their social status, could find a family that would more than willingly welcome them to their table. Even today, many Jewish families actively seek out someone to invite home to share their fare.

Two pragmatic problems arose from the tradition. The first was that one could never know when or how many guests might descend for dinner and the second was that most shtetl families were barely able to sustain themselves. There simply was not that much food to go around. The solution to both problems was simple enough: so long as the family could afford one very large pot, there could always be a soup available for anyone who could possibly be hungry at any time. The byword of many Jewish homes became: *Let them eat soup.*

There were several requirements that fell on such soups. They had to be hardy — that is to say, the guest had to feel both full and satisfied after a meal. They had to have both bulk and nutrition, and, if one prefers, there had to be a large quantity of soup available. Because of the exigencies of daily life, the soups had to be simple and economical to prepare. But most of all, they had to be tasty, for nothing could be more catastrophic than to have a guest leave and spread the word that the food he had been served was not quite up to snuff. In villages the physical and social size of the shtetls, the word spread quickly. It wasn't so much a matter of keeping up with the wealthy Pugatch family as of letting it be known that Reb Asher enjoyed his meal with the impoverished Snitkoffs.

Whether for guests or not, soups have remained an important staple in the Yiddish kitchen and the soups associated with that cuisine have remained true to their origins. The basic ingredients are generally available year round, are not overly expensive, can be made in large quantities, can be reheated and enjoyed even several nights after cooking, and are as tasty a fare as one might wish to find. The one rule is simple enough: if it grows in or on the earth, fits in a pot, and maintains its flavour after being cooked, it will make a good soup.

D.G.

Borscht

Running a close second in popularity to Chicken Soup, Russian Borscht, in any of its multitude of forms, provides an excellent soup or mid-day refresher served either hot or cold and garnished with an assortment ranging from sour cream, boiled potatoes, sliced hard boiled eggs or parsley. As someone once put it, "there are probably as many versions of this particular soup as there are Jews."

Borscht — 1

2 cups beets, peeled and chopped finely
2 cups beef or chicken stock
1 cup cabbage, shredded finely
1 cup onions, chopped finely
½ cup carrots, chopped finely
2 tblspns butter
juice of 1 lemon
sour cream for garnish

1. In a large kettle place the beets, onions and carrots and barely cover these with boiling water. On a moderate flame simmer these gently, covered, for 20 minutes. Add the remaining ingredients, recover and simmer for 15 minutes longer. Pour into individual bowls and garnish each portion with 1 tblspn sour cream.

Serves 6.

Borscht — 2

3½ lbs (1½ kilo) beets, trimmed
3 tsp sugar
1 tblspn salt
juice of 1 lemon

1. Clean the beets thoroughly and peel. Cut in pieces and place these in a large saucepan with 8 cups cold water. Bring to a boil and then reduce flame cooking, covered, until beets are softened half through. Add remaining ingredients, cover again and allow to cook until beets are soft through. Strain the borscht, allow to cool 15-20 minutes and refrigerate, covered. Serve cold either in glasses or bowls. If desired, garnish each portion with 1 tblspn sour cream.

Serves 6.

Borscht — 3

2 lbs (900 gr) beets, peeled
1 lb (450 gr) chicken wings and necks
2 carrots
2 medium onions
2 stalks celery
1 tblspn salt
juice of 1 lemon
½ tsp pepper

1. In a large kettle place the beets, onions and carrots. On these lay the chicken pieces and remaining ingredients. Cover with 8 cups water and, on moderately high flame, bring to a boil. Allow to boil for 10 minutes and then reduce flame, cover and simmer for 2 hours. Check periodically and add water if necessary.
2. Remove from heat, adjust seasoning and strain the soup. May be served hot or cold and garnished either with sour cream, boiled potatoes, parsley or hard-boiled eggs.

Serves 6.

Schav — Sour Grass Soup

1 lb (450 gr) sour grass
6 spring onions, chopped coarsely
1 cup sour cream
2 eggs
juice of 3 lemons, strained
1½ tsp salt
1 tsp sugar
½ tsp black pepper

1. Wash the sour grass thoroughly and chop coarsely. Place these in a large saucepan with the spring onions and 4 cups cold water. Add the salt, pepper and sugar, stir well and bring to a boil. Reduce the flame, add the lemon juice and simmer, covered, on medium-low flame for 30 minutes, until the grass is completely tender. Remove from flame and allow to cool.
2. Beat the eggs in a bowl and gradually add in 1 cup of the cool broth, stirring

constantly. Add this mixture to the soup slowly, stirring constantly. Refrigerate until just before serving and then mix in the sour cream, stirring well until completely blended. Serve cold.

Serves 4-6.

Spinach Soup with Sour Cream

2 lbs (900 gr) spinach leaves
5 spring onions, chopped coarsely
1 cup sour cream
2 eggs
juice of 2 lemons
2 tsp salt
¾ tsp sugar

1. Wash spinach leaves thoroughly. Chop the spinach and place in a large saucepan with the spring onions and 6 cups cold water. Add the salt, stir well and bring to a boil. Reduce the heat and add the lemon juice and sugar. Cover and allow to simmer on medium-low flame 20 minutes. Remove from flame and allow to cool.
2. Beat the eggs in a bowl and gradually add in 1 cup of the cool broth, stirring constantly. Add this mixture to the soup slowly, stirring constantly. Refrigerate until just before serving and then mix in the sour cream, stirring well until completely blended. Serve cold.

Serves 6.

Cabbage and Beef Soup

1½ lbs (675 gr) soup bones with meat
1 lb (450 gr) sauerkraut
2 cups cabbage, shredded
½ cup tomato juice
2 onions, chopped
3 apples, peeled, cored and cubed
4 tblspns chicken fat
juice of 2 lemons
2 tblspns sugar
1 tsp black pepper
salt to taste

1. In a heavy saucepan heat the fat and sauté the onions until golden brown. Add the meat and sauté until browned on all sides. Add remaining bones (if any), cabbage, sauerkraut, tomato juice and 2 quarts (2 litres) water. Bring to a boil and allow to boil for 3-5 minutes, skimming the foam from the surface. Lower flame, cover and simmer for 2 hours.

2. Add remaining ingredients, recover and simmer 45 minutes longer. Serve hot.

Serves 6-8.

Sweet and Sour Cabbage Soup

1 medium head cabbage
1 lb (450 gr) rib meat
1 cup tomato sauce
1 medium onion, sliced
2 tblspns each brown sugar and sour salts
1 tblspn white sugar
1 tsp salt
½ tsp pepper

1. Cut the cabbage into eighths and put into large saucepan. Add the meat and 5 cups water. Cook, uncovered, on medium flame for ½ hour. Add remaining ingredients, cover and continue cooking on low flame for 1½-2 hours. Serve hot.

Serves 4-6.

Mushroom and Barley Soup

1 lb (450 gr) soup meat with bones
¾ cup dried lima beans
½ cup dried mushrooms
1 cup barley
2 onions, chopped
1 carrot, peeled and sliced
3 tblspns chicken fat
salt and pepper to taste

1. Soak the beans in water overnight. Drain and rinse the beans and set aside. Soak the mushrooms in water 1 hour.

2. In a large kettle place the meat and bones and add 2 quarts (2 litres) water. Over a high flame bring to a rapid boil. Remove the foam from the surface, add the lima beans, reduce flame, cover and simmer for 1 hour.

3. In a skillet melt the chicken fat and sauté the onions until golden brown. Add these to the kettle. Drain the mushrooms and add to the kettle with the barley and carrot. Add salt and pepper to taste, bring to a boil again and then simmer, covered, 1 hour. Adjust seasonings and serve hot.

Serves 8.

Barley Soup

1 lb (450 gr) chicken wings and necks
6 cups beef stock (page 78)
1 cup each celery and carrot, diced
1 onion, chopped coarsely
2 tblspns parsley, chopped
1 cup barley
2 tsp salt
½ tsp black pepper

1. Place the ingredients in a large saucepan or kettle along with 2 cups cold water. Over a high flame bring to a boil. Reduce heat and let simmer, uncovered, 1 hour or until barley is tender. Correct seasoning and simmer 10 minutes longer. Serve hot.

Serves 6.

Bean Soup

2 lbs (900 gr) marrow bones
1 cup dried white beans
3 small potatoes, peeled and quartered
2 carrots, sliced
2 medium onions
1 small celery root, cleaned
salt and pepper to taste

1. Soak beans in water overnight. Drain and rinse the beans and place them in large saucepan with the marrow bones. Add cold water to cover. On a high

flame bring to a rapid boil and skim the foam from the surface. Cover, reduce flame and simmer for 2½ hours.

2. Add remaining ingredients, bring soup to a boil again and allow to boil 1 - 2 minutes. Reduce heat and simmer, uncovered, for 1 hour. Discard onion and celery root before serving. Serve with the bones.

Serves 4-6.

Potato Soup

1 cup milk
4 large potatoes, peeled and diced
1 large carrot, sliced
1 onion, whole
1 parsnip, whole
3 stalks celery, halved
1 tblspn butter
salt and pepper to taste

1. Place all ingredients except butter and milk in a large saucepan and add 2 cups water. On a high flame bring to a boil and let boil 1 - 2 minutes. Lower flame, cover, and let simmer until potatoes are soft (about ½ hour).

2. With a slotted spoon remove and discard onion, celery and parsnip. Add the milk and butter and reheat. Serve hot.

Serves 4.

Potato-Leek Soup

4 medium potatoes, peeled and sliced
4 leeks, sliced in rounds
2½ cups milk
2½ tblspns butter
salt and pepper to taste

1. In a large saucepan put the potatoes, leeks, 2 cups cold water and salt and pepper to taste. Bring to a boil and immediately cover, allowing to boil rapidly for 2-3 minutes. Lower flame and simmer until potatoes are soft (about 20 minutes). Adjust seasonings, add the milk and butter and heat through. Serve hot.

Serves 4.

Cauliflower Soup

1 large head cauliflower
½ lb (225 gr) potatoes, peeled
1 cup milk
4 tsp butter
salt and pepper to taste
dash nutmeg

1. Clean the cauliflower well and separate into flowerettes. Put these in a large saucepan and add 6 cups cold water, salt and pepper to taste. Bring to a boil and cover, lowering flame and simmering until just tender (10 - 15 minutes). Remove the cauliflower with a slotted spoon and reserve.
2. Quarter the potatoes and add them to the broth. Bring to a boil, reduce flame and simmer, covered, until potatoes are soft.
3. Set several whole flowerettes aside and add the remaining cauliflower to the broth. Add the milk and mash the vegetables into the mixture. Adjust the seasoning and blend the mixture well (by hand or in blender). Return to the saucepan, add reserved flowerettes and reheat, but do not boil. Serve hot with a pat of butter floating on each serving and sprinkled with the nutmeg.

Serves 6.

Cold Cucumber Soup

6 large cucumbers
1 large pickled cucumber
1 cup heavy sweet cream
2 tblspns tarragon vinegar
¼ tsp garlic powder
1 cup yoghurt
2 tblspns chopped mint leaves
salt and pepper to taste

1. Wash cucumbers and grate coarsely (do not peel).
2. Combine the yoghurt and cream. To this add remaining ingredients, mix and chill well. Serve cold, adding the chopped mint by sprinkling over individual portions immediately prior to serving.

Serves 6.

Goulash Soup

¾ lb (350 gr) goulash beef, cubed
3 large potatoes, peeled and cubed
3 medium onions, chopped coarsely
3 medium tomatoes, skinned and mashed
2 large green peppers, chopped coarsely
¼ cup tomato purée
3 tblspns chicken fat
1 tsp sweet paprika
½ tsp each dill seed and black pepper
¼ tsp marjoram
salt and hot paprika to taste
dumplings (following)

1. In a large saucepan melt the fat and sauté the onions and green peppers until soft. Add the beef and sauté until browned on all sides. Add the tomatoes, tomato purée diluted in ¼ cup water, sweet paprika, marjoram, dill, salt, pepper and hot paprika. Add 1 quart (1 litre) water and, on medium-low flame, simmer for 1 hour. Correct seasonings, add the potatoes and simmer 1 hour longer. Add the dumplings just before serving.

Serves 4-6.

Dumplings

Dumplings, regardless of whether they are made of basic flour, potato or matzo meal are delicious served with goulash or goulash soup. They also make superb accompaniment to clear soups or any meat with a tangy sauce.

Matzo Meal Dumplings

1 cup matzo meal
6 eggs
5 tblspns oil
1½ tsp salt
pinch each ginger and nutmeg

1. In a mixing bowl combine the oil, eggs and seasonings. Gradually add the

matzo meal and mix until the dough is firm. Cover and let stand 1 - 2 hours.

2. Wet the hands and form the dough into balls about 1½" (4 cm) in diameter. In a saucepan boil a large amount of lightly salted water. Bring to a gentle boil and into this gently place the dumplings. Reduce flame and allow to simmer 20 minutes.

Flour Dumplings

½ lb (225 gr) flour
¼ cup oil
2 eggs
1 tsp salt
¼ tsp white pepper

1. In a large bowl mix well the oil, ½ cup water, eggs and seasonings. Gradually, and alternately, add the flour and enough water to yield a dough that is soft but not overly thin.

2. In a large saucepan boil a large amount of water with 1 tsp each salt and oil. While the water is boiling rapidly drop small bits of dough straight into the boiling water. Stir nearly constantly with wooden spoon and allow to cook 10 minutes. Remove dumplings from the water and rinse in cold running water. Transfer dumplings to a bowl with 1 tblspn oil and toss well.

Potato Dumplings

2 lbs (900 gr) potatoes, peeled
1 cup flour
2 eggs, beaten
salt and pepper to taste

1. In a saucepan with boiling salted water cook half the potatoes until soft. Drain and mash.

2. Grate coarsely the remaining potatoes and squeeze out the excess fluid. Mash together the cooked and grated potatoes and add remaining ingredients, mixing well. Form into ½" (1 cm) balls and drop these gently into a large saucepan with boiling salted water. When dumplings rise to the surface cover and boil 10 minutes longer.

Lamb Soup

1½ lbs (675 gr) boneless lamb
¾ lb (350 gr) marrow bones
2 carrots, sliced
2 medium onions, quartered
2 stalks celery, quartered
2 sprigs parsley
¾ tsp dried dill weed
salt and pepper to taste

1. In a large saucepan place the meat, bones and 2 quarts (2 litres) cold water. Cover and boil gently for 1 hour, skimming off foam occasionally. Add the remaining ingredients, bring to a boil and then reduce flame and simmer, covered, until meat is tender (about 45 minutes). Remove the celery and parsley before serving. Serve hot.

Serves 8.

Chicken Stock

3½ lbs (1½ kilo) chicken necks, wings, backs and feet
6 whole peppercorns
6 whole cloves
6 parsley stems
1 medium onion, diced
3 stalks celery, diced
1 bay leaf
1 tsp thyme

1. Place the chicken parts in a colander and pour over them several quarts (litres) of hot water. Afterwards rinse the parts in cold water.
2. To a large saucepan with 4 quarts (4 litres) of water, add the chicken parts and all remaining ingredients. Bring to a boil and immediately reduce the flame and let simmer 2½ - 3 hours or until reduced by half. Strain the stock and allow to cool, uncovered, before covering and refrigerating to store.

Yields about 2 quarts (2 litres) stock.

Beef Stock

6 lbs (3 kilo) shin and marrow bones
5 medium tomatoes, whole
3 stalks celery, diced
3 sprigs parsley
1 large onion, diced
1 small white turnip, diced
1 large carrot, diced
10 whole peppercorns
6 whole cloves
2 bay leaves
1 tsp thyme

1. To a large saucepan or kettle with 4 quarts (4 litres) of water, add all the ingredients and bring to a boil. Reduce heat and simmer uncovered for about 2½ hours or until reduced by half. Strain the stock and allow to cool, uncovered, before covering and refrigerating to store.

Yields about 2 quarts (2 litres) stock.

The Rules of the Game

Thou shalt not bear false witness.
Exodus 13:13

JEWISH COOKS are not normally liars. While they are fully capable of embellishing tales with a magnificent flourish or spinning yarns as intricate as any storyteller might desire, they usually avoid out-and-out lies. It is simply too embarrassing to be caught.

The men of the species enjoy exaggerating reports of their status, real or imagined, in their professions and also derive pleasure from implying, albeit never directly, masterful sexual potency and techniques. The women gain an almost orgasmic pleasure in exaggerating the burdens placed on them by their husbands, children, in-laws, and other family members. Parents of either sex enjoy stretching, sometimes to the point of complete unbelievability, stories dealing with the intelligence, wit and charm of their children. Such complaints and tales are so common that few listen in the first place and no one is overly concerned about validity.

But when it comes to their recipes, most Jewish cooks cross the line and become just plain liars. Jews are simply not to be relied upon when it comes to sharing the secrets of their culinary success.

Being asked to share a recipe implies either a compliment or a politeness. That is to say, those people who enjoyed the meal truly want the recipe and those who did not enjoy it are embarrassed to say so. This puts the cook in an untenable position, for if they do share their favourite recipe it only means that Cousin Shmulik or Tante Rozelle will be able to make it just as well at the next family dinner. This is not perceived as desirable as it will detract from the uniqueness of the chef who has been called upon to divulge his or her secrets. The solution to this is really rather simple: the recipe is given but it either lacks a critical ingredient or another has been added that will almost guarantee an unpalatable result. Such deception may be thought of as having malicious intent.

A second problem affects even those cooks who really would like to share their recipes. The complication that frequently arises is that many Jewish cooks operate not so much on the concept of fixed amounts with regard to ingredients as they do on a sense of "feel". One adds a *shnipple* (a bit) of this, a *bissle* (a littler bit) of that and a *shtick* (a somewhat larger bit) of that . . . Simply stated, many really excellent cooks do not *know* how much of anything went into their dishes. To admit this is embarrassing, so there are those who simply make up amounts as they come to mind. This, the lesser of the sins, may be thought of as deceit by default or embarrassment.

Fortunately for most chefs, such perjury is neither as morally or legally complicated as that which takes place in a court of law. No less luckily for most offenders, they are rarely caught, and this for two reasons. First, most of the people who take the recipes are also Jewish cooks who cannot prepare any recipe without just a bit of personal improvisation. Second, regardless of whether the new owner of the recipe improvises or not, failure will generally be taken personally and no blame attaches to the donor.

Other rules of the Jewish kitchen apply primarily to the eater and not to the cook. It is *de rigueur*, for example, before the meal for guests to venture at least once into the kitchen and there to loudly proclaim how the aromas of the food under preparation are quite enough to drive one mad with hunger.

More important than this, it is important for guests to realize that one's host or hostess will never be satisfied if meals have been described as "pleasant" or "nice". No compliment couched in terms less than superlative will suffice. Comments about meals that are less than "superb" or "magnificent" will be taken with offense serious enough to trigger family feuds that may endure for a generation or more. At best, although guests will be spared the sarcastic comments that are reserved for family members, they will not be able to avoid pained or reproachful glances for their inappropriate behaviour.

One should not, however, be overly daunted by all of this. It should be remembered that most of those who prepare Jewish meals do it with a handsome amount of skill and a healthy modicum of love. From these come meals that may indeed be spoken of in terms of superlatives. As for those meals that will have proven only "quite good" rather than excellent, a few white lies in the sake of pleasing the cook never hurt anyone.

D.G.

Katze Putze mit Grutze

Why does man kill? He kills for food. And not only for food: frequently there must be a beverage.

Woody Allen

AS ONE HAS progressed through our little book, by now two things (at least) have become obvious: that it is considered absolutely necessary in the Jewish home to put more on the table than can possibly be consumed and that one should never waste food. Despite a seeming opposition in logic, these two injunctions are not in the least bit contradictory.

Perhaps the best way of dealing with this philosophical dilemma is by explaining, at least to that extent which one may decently do in public, the behaviour of my mother.

A master in the kitchen, not only was the food she prepared invariably tasty but was always presented with just the correct amounts of love, suffering and agony that should accompany Jewish food. Despite economic ups and downs, there was always plenty to eat and everyone in the family had more than a few favourite dishes.

At least once a week there was a delicate chicken soup. No matter how much we ate there was still more in the pot. Every week also found our table set with at least one other soup as well, barley, bean and lamb being among the household favourites. From these too there was an overage. There would be one meal of either chopped meat or meat loaf, either having been prepared in amounts adequate to feed a hungry horde rather than a moderate-sized family. Another meal would be primarily of vegetables, possibly including potato pancakes or a kugel. From this too there were leftovers. At least one dinner would consist primarily of a baked or roasted beef that seemed, at least to us, adequate in size to feed the entire neighbourhood.

My younger brother and I never really wondered what happened to all those leftovers. To us what was important was that there was enough and that it tasted good. So much for the desires of young children.

One of the meals to which we looked forward enormously was that which our mother called *katze putze mit grutze*, the regular Thursday night feature at our home. It was reported (at least by our parents) that we were fairly bright kids. That report may, however, be disregarded. Despite a fair knowledge of Yiddish it took us until we were nearly ten years old to realize that our beloved *katze putze* was nothing more than a magnificent casserole composed of all the leftovers of the week. How that combination of beef, chicken, sauces, vegetables, potatoes and seasonings managed to taste quite so delicious remained quite a mystery until my own adult years. I am glad, however, to report that my own daughter proved a bit wiser in this affair. By the time she was six she would tease by requesting: "Daddy . . . this week maybe we could have the katze putze *without* the grutze?"

D.R.

Baked Beef

3½ lbs (1½ kilo) brisket beef
4 medium tomatoes, in eighths
1 large onion, chopped coarsely
2 sweet red peppers, quartered
¾ cup dry white wine
3 tblspns oil
½ tsp each salt and black pepper
hot paprika to taste

1. In a skillet heat the oil and in this sauté the onions until golden brown. To this add the beef stirring well to assure that the beef is well coated by the oil and then add an amount of water to half-cover the beef. Add the salt, pepper and paprika, cover and allow to simmer on a low flame until the meat is half done (about ¾ hour).

2. Remove the meat from the skillet, cool slightly and cut into cubes. Place these in an ovenproof casserole and add the peppers, tomatoes, fried onions and the liquid in which the meat was cooked. Cover and place in medium oven until meat is soft. When the meat is ready remove the cover, pour over the wine and place back in oven until meat is well browned on top. Serve hot.

Serves 6-8.

Baked Beef in Wine Sauce

1 4-lb (1¾ kilo) roast beef, cubed
1 cup red wine
1 cup baby or white onions, whole
1 cup small mushrooms, whole
4 medium potatoes, peeled and quartered
½ cup each tomato sauce and flour
½ cup each onions and carrots, diced
2 cloves garlic, chopped
1 bay leaf
salt and pepper to taste
oil for frying

1. In a skillet heat the oil and sauté the meat until browned on all sides. Remove the meat to a casserole. In the oil sauté the onions and carrots until onions

become slightly golden. Transfer to the casserole and add the flour, diced onions and carrots, garlic, tomato sauce, seasonings, red wine and water to just cover.

2. Cook, tightly closed, in a medium oven for 2 hours. Do not allow to boil. Add the onions, mushrooms and potatoes and cook, uncovered, 40 minutes longer. Serve hot.

Serves 6-8.

Cholent

If there is an ultimately Jewish dish, it is cholent. Because cholent requires a particularly long cooking time it was ideal for preparation on Friday afternoon, before the onset of the Sabbath and for dining on the following day when cooking was prohibited.

4½ lbs (2 kilo) potatoes
2 lbs (900 gr) brisket beef
2 lbs (900 gr) stuffed kishke (page 87)
1 lb (450 gr) chicken fat
3 cups white beans
1 cup pearl barley
2 large onions, chopped
2 tsp each salt and black pepper
1 tsp paprika
oil for frying

1. Soak the beans in water overnight.
2. Sauté the onions in hot oil until golden. Peel and cut the potatoes in quarters. Cut beef into 2" (5 cm) cubes.
3. Grease a large heavy saucepan or kettle. Arrange in this layers of potatoes, barley, beans and chicken fat. Add the seasonings. Repeat layers until ingredients have been used. On this lay the beef and over this put the kishke. Over this spoon the fried onions. Fill the pot with water to cover the ingredients and bring to a boil over a high flame. Cover and seal the pot (with aluminum foil perhaps). Place in oven at lowest heat. Cholent will be ready to eat after 18 hours but will be at its best after 24 hours. Serve hot.

Serves 8-12.

Lamb Cholent

3 lbs (1½ kilo) potatoes
2 lbs (900 gr) lamb or mutton cubes
2 lbs (900 gr) kishke (following)
1½ cups pearl barley
½ lb (225 gr) chicken fat
2 large onions, chopped
1½ tsp each salt and pepper
1 tsp paprika
oil for frying

1. Soak the beans in water overnight.
2. Sauté onions in oil until golden. Peel and cut the potatoes in quarters. Cut the lamb into 2" (5 cm) cubes.
3. Grease a large heavy saucepan or kettle. Arrange in it layers of potatoes, barley and beans. Repeat layers until these ingredients have been used up. On top of this place the chicken fat and then add the seasonings and lay on the meat. Spoon over this the fried onions. Fill with water to cover and bring to a boil over high flame. Cover and seal the pot (with aluminum foil perhaps). Place in oven at lowest heat. Cook 18-24 hours. Serve hot.

Serves 8-12.

Stuffed Derma — Kishke

3 feet (1 metre) beef casing
1 cup flour
¼ cup dried bread crumbs
½ cup chicken fat
1 large onion, chopped finely
salt and pepper to taste

1. Wash and clean the casing thoroughly, scraping off fat with dull knife and discarding. Cut into lengths about 8" (20 cm) and sew one end of each length.
2. In a skillet melt the chicken fat and sauté the onions until browned.
3. In a mixing bowl, sift together the flour, salt and pepper. Add the melted chicken fat with the onions, the bread crumbs and mix thoroughly. Stuff each section of the casing loosely with this filling and sew the second end closed. Rinse off any flour that may adhere to the surface. Immerse in boiling water for 5 minutes and then drain.

4. Arrange the sections in a shallow, lightly greased casserole or baking dish and bake in medium oven 1½ hours or until well browned, basing frequently with the drippings.

Note: This is a recipe for preparing kishke itself. If it is to be served with cholent follow steps 1 - 3 only and then stew overnight with the cholent as described (page 86).

Serves 6.

Boiled Beef with Potatoes

2 lbs (900 gr) beef brisket
1 lb (450 gr) potatoes, peeled and quartered
4 carrots, quartered
4 medium onions, whole
2 stalks celery with leaves, halved
salt and pepper to taste
prepared horseradish or horseradish sauce (page 52)

1. In a large saucepan boil 2 quarts (2 litres) water and add the meat. Bring to a boil again while removing foam from surface. Add vegetables, salt and pepper and simmer, covered, 1 hour.

2. Add the potatoes to the saucepan, recover and simmer 35 minutes longer (or until potatoes are soft through). Remove the meat from the broth and allow to cool. Cut into slices and serve on a large platter with the potatoes, whole onions and carrots. Garnish with horseradish or horseradish sauce.

Serves 4.

Brisket of Beef in Wine

1 3½-lb (1½ kilo) brisket of beef
1 cup dry red wine
½ cup lemon juice
¼ cup oil
2 onions, chopped coarsely
1 carrot, chopped
4 cloves garlic, chopped
1½ tsp salt
1 tsp black pepper
¾ tsp sugar

1. Combine all of the ingredients, except the beef, and mix thoroughly.
2. Place the meat in a roasting pan and pour over it the marinade, turning the meat until well coated on all sides. Cover the pan and refrigerate, turning the meat occasionally, for 12-16 hours.
3. Place the roast, tightly covered, in a medium oven and let cook 3-3½ hours or until meat is tender. Remove the meat to a serving platter and from the liquid skim off excess fat. Reheat the sauce and serve in sauceboat. Serve hot.

Serves 4-6.

Pot Roast of Beef

1 beef shoulder, about 5 lbs (2¼ kilo), tied
1 lb (450 gr) carrots, halved
1 lb (450 gr) potatoes, peeled and halved
1 lb (450 gr) green beans, trimmed
7 medium onions, whole
3 cups beef stock (page 78)
¾ cup tomato purée
½ cup oil
6 sprigs parsley
2 stalks celery
2 cloves garlic, chopped
1 bay leaf
3 tblspns flour
1½ tsp salt
¾ tsp black pepper

1. Sprinkle the beef with the flour. In a large kettle or saucepan heat the oil and in this brown the meat well on all sides. Remove the beef from the kettle and set aside. Slice one onion and fry in the hot oil until golden brown. Place the beef back in the kettle and add the stock, salt, pepper, tomato purée, celery, garlic, parsley and bay leaf. Bring to a boil and then reduce flame, cover and simmer gently for 2 hours.
2. Arrange the remaining vegetables in the kettle, cover and continue to simmer 1 hour longer. Discard the celery, bay leaf and parsley and taste the juices, adjusting seasonings if necessary. Remove the meat from the kettle. Discard tying strings and excess fat. Surround the meat with the cooked vegetables.

3. Strain the sauce into a 2-quart (2 litre) saucepan. Bring to a boil and boil until reduced by half. Immediately before serving pour over a small amount of the sauce on the meat. Serve remaining sauce in a sauceboat. Serve hot.

Serves 8-10.

Pot Roast — Sauerbraten

3½ lbs (1½ kilo) beef shoulder
2 cups dry red wine
2 onions, grated coarsely
10 whole cloves
3 cloves garlic, chopped
6 tblspns matzo meal
4 tblspns oil
1 tsp each salt and sugar
½ tsp black pepper

1. Mix together the wine, onions, garlic, ½ tsp salt, cloves and 1 cup water. Place the meat in a large container and over this pour the marinade. Cover and refrigerate for 24 hours, turning occasionally.
2. Mix together the matzo meal, pepper and remaining salt. Remove the meat from the marinade and rub well with this mixture. Strain and reserve the marinade.
3. In a heavy saucepan heat the oil and, over a high flame, sear the meat on all sides. Add 1 cup strained marinade and 1 cup water and bring to a boil. Cover, reduce flame and simmer until meat is tender (about 1½ hours). Add additional water and marinade in equal parts only if pot becomes dry.

Serves 6.

Hungarian Goulash

3½ lbs (1½ kilo) goulash meat, cubed
5 medium onions, chopped
2 green peppers, chopped
2 tomatoes, chopped
3 oz (100 gr) tomato purée
salt and hot paprika to taste
oil for frying

1. Heat the oil in a large skillet. Sauté the chopped onions until golden brown. Add the meat and sauté until well browned. Add the peppers, tomatoes, salt and paprika and 6 tblspns water. Stir with a wooden spoon, cover and cook on low flame until meat is soft (about 2 hours). Add a small quantity of water periodically so that the sauce remains thick but not sticky. Serve hot.

2. Serving recommendation: On each portion spoon one dollop of sour cream and spread dumplings (page 75) generously.

Serves 6.

Russian Goulash

3½ lbs (1½ kilo) goulash meat, in large cubes
3 onions, sliced
3 oz (100 gr) tomato purée
2 hot red peppers, chopped finely
4 tblspns chopped parsley
¾ tsp each salt and dill seed
½ tsp black pepper

1. In a saucepan cover the meat just barely with water. Add the onions, red peppers, salt, pepper and dill weed. Cook, uncovered, on a low flame for about 2 hours, stirring occasionally until meat is soft.

2. Transfer the meat to a large skillet and add the tomato purée, parsley and ½ cup of the cooking liquid. On a medium flame, stirring, heat until sauce thickens. Serve hot.

Serves 4-6.

Sweet and Sour Stew — Essik Fleish

3½ lbs (1½ kilo) stewing meat, cubed
¾ cup seedless raisins
2 onions, finely chopped
2 tblspns each vinegar and brown sugar
2 tblspns tomato purée
3 garlic cloves, finely chopped
2 bay leaves
salt and pepper to taste
oil for frying

1. In a heavy saucepan sauté the onions and garlic in hot oil until golden brown. Add the meat and continue sautéeing until brown on all sides.

2. Mix together the remaining ingredients with 1½ cups water and pour over the meat. Bring to a boil, reduce flame and simmer, covered, for 2 hours. Serve over cooked broad noodles.

Serves 4-6.

Stewed Calf's Liver with Onions

2 lbs (900 gr) calf's liver
8 medium onions, chopped coarsely
4 medium potatoes, peeled and sliced
4 medium apples, peeled, cored and sliced
2 cups beef stock (page 78)
6 tblspns chicken fat
salt and pepper to taste
pinch oregano

1. In a large heavy skillet sauté the onions in half the fat until golden brown. Remove onions from skillet with slotted spoon and set aside.

2. Season the liver with salt and pepper and cut into 1-2″ (2½-5 cm) slices. Heat the remaining fat in the skillet and in this sauté the liver, browning both sides. Add the remaining ingredients, cover and simmer on low flame for 30 minutes or until liver is done. Serve hot.

Serves 4-6.

Tongue in Wine Sauce

4½ lbs (2 kilo) pickled tongue
3 cups beef stock (page 78)
1 cup port wine
10 whole peppercorns
9 bay leaves
1 tblspn butter
1 tblspn cornflour
2 tsp dill weed
1 tsp sweet paprika

1. Remove the fatty end of the tongue and reserve for future use in soup or

stew. Place the tongue in a large pot and cover with water. Add 5 bay leaves, the peppercorns and the dill seed. Cook for about 2 hours or until tongue is soft. Peel under cold running water and allow to cool.

2. Boil the wine with 4 bay leaves in a saucepan until the wine is reduced by half. Remove from the flame. Add the butter and paprika, mixing well. While the sauce is still hot, thicken by adding and mixing well 1 tblspn cornflour.

3. Slice the tongue thinly and heat in the sauce. Serve hot.

Serves 8.

Stuffed Veal Breast

3½ lbs (1½ kilo) breast of veal
1½ cups uncooked kashe (buckwheat groats)
½ cup dry white or red wine
2 medium onions, chopped
3 slices white bread, without crusts
4 cloves garlic, chopped finely
4 tblspns butter
1 tsp sweet paprika
salt and pepper to taste

1. In a saucepan melt 2 tblspns butter and in this sauté the garlic until just brown.

2. Cut a pocket in the veal breast and brush inside and out of the breast with the garlic-butter mixture. Sprinkle the outside of the veal with the paprika.

3. In the skillet melt the remaining butter and in this sauté the onions until golden brown. Add the kashe and stir constantly until kashe is thoroughly coated with the butter, about 3-4 minutes. Crumb the white bread and add this, the salt and pepper and ¾ cup water to the skillet. Reduce heat, cover and simmer until kashe is soft (about 15 minutes).

4. Stuff the kashe mixture into the pocket and place in an ovenproof casserole. Place in low oven, covered, for 2 hours. Remove cover, and continue to bake, basting occasionally with the natural juices for an additional 40 minutes.

5. Remove the veal to serving platter. To the juices add the wine, between ¼-½ cup water, and stir well. Adjust seasoning with salt and pepper and pour over the stuffed breast. Serve hot.

Serves 6-8.

Stuffed Cabbage Leaves — 1

1 large head cabbage
1 lb (450 gr) ground beef
¾ cup tomato purée
3 onions, chopped finely
½ cup half cooked rice
1½ tblspns brown sugar
juice of 1 lemon
1 egg, well beaten
½ tsp sweet paprika
½ tsp ground nutmeg
salt and pepper to taste
oil for frying

1. In a skillet heat the oil and sauté the onions until golden and transfer to a mixing dish with the ground beef, rice, egg, nutmeg, salt and pepper. Mix thoroughly.
2. Core the cabbage. Trim and separate leaves and put leaves in boiling, salted water for 3-5 minutes. Drain. At the top edge of each leaf place 2 tablespoons of the stuffing. Roll the leaves while tucking in the sides.
3. In a separate bowl mix the tomato paste, lemon juice, sugar, and paprika. Add 2 cups cold water, adjust seasonings. Place the stuffed leaves in a large saucepan and pour over the sauce. Bring to a boil, reduce heat and simmer, covered, 2 hours. Serve hot.

Serves 4-6.

Stuffed Cabbage Leaves — 2

1 large head of cabbage
1 lb (450 gr) ground beef
2 cups cooked rice
½ cup seedless raisins
1½ cups tomato sauce
1 cup chicken stock (page 77)
3 medium onions, chopped
3 tblspns parsley, chopped
2 cloves garlic, chopped
2 bay leaves
1 tsp salt
½ tsp each pepper and thyme
oil for frying

1. In a large skillet heat the oil and sauté the onions and garlic until onions are translucent. Add the ground beef and continue sautéeing until well browned. Add the rice, raisins, parsley, thyme, salt, pepper and ⅓ cup of tomato sauce. Mix thoroughly and simmer 5 minutes.

2. Core the cabbage. Trim and separate leaves and put leaves in boiling, salted water for 3-5 minutes. Drain. At the top edge of each leaf place 2 tablespoons of the stuffing. Roll the leaves while tucking in the sides.

3. In a saucepan combine the remaining ingredients and bring to a boil. Remove the bay leaf and pour the sauce over the cabbage rolls in an ovenproof casserole. Bake, uncovered, in medium oven, for 1 hour. Serve hot.

Serves 4-6.

The Kosher Chicken

These are the living things which ye may eat . . .
Leviticus 11:2

BEING JEWISH has never been easy. The Torah lists a total of 613 injunctions: 365 as to what we shall not do and 248 concerning what we must do. Some of those injunctions (*mitzvot*) concern themselves with the relationship between man and God; others deal with how men and women individually and collectively should relate to each other. It is difficult enough to learn the rules but it is even harder to abide by them. It becomes even more complex when one realizes that some of these injunctions relate to chickens.

Chickens are important to Jews. While they are alive they give eggs and serve as alarm clocks. They also give feathers, although no one, Jewish or other, has found a particularly valuable use for chicken feathers. Chickens also give us soup, chicken fat, *griebens*, and of course, meat. Between roasting, baking, frying, boiling, poaching and grilling, the chicken proves a versatile bird indeed. Unfortunately for the chicken, its greatest versatility is found only after its death. This, while it proves an enormous problem for chickens, gives Jews quite a headache as well.

According to the laws of *kashrut* (the dietary laws), one may not eat the meat of an animal which has died from disease, old age or accident. Accidents to chickens are not of major concern so long as one takes even the most basic precautions such as not allowing one's chicken to have driving licenses. Death from old age is another story however, for when considering the enormous value of eggs, it pays to keep chickens alive and laying for as long as possible. The wise chicken owner must therefore play a well-informed game of chance on ensuring that the chicken will be slaughtered before it demises on its own volition.

Another injunction that applies to the relationship between Jews and chickens is that which prohibits any form of cruelty to animals. According to these rules every animal must be slaughtered by a *shochet* (ritual slaughterer) who is well trained in ensuring that the animal will suffer as quick and painless a death as possible. The dilemma of how any creature may be "slaughtered" humanely, while it has not driven too many Jews to vegetarianism, has served as a source for a modicum of guilt over many a bowl of otherwise delicious chicken soup.

Within the last decade a new problem has arisen. Whether chickens that are fertilized, hatched and raised from the process of cloning will or will not prove to be "real" chickens according to the many biblical injunctions will surely provide food for thought for Talmudic scholars for the next several generations. Whether such new-breed chicks will provide food for the kosher household remains open to their findings.

D.L.

Baked Stuffed Chicken

1 medium chicken
½ lb (225 gr) ground beef
4 tblspns half-cooked rice
4 tblspns chopped parsley
¼ cup dried bread crumbs
2 oz (50 gr) chopped almonds
rind of 1 lemon, grated
½ tsp each salt and pepper
¼ tsp each rosemary and tarragon
sweet paprika to taste
oil for basting

1. Clean the chicken well, trimming and discarding excess fat. Sprinkle the chicken, inside and out, with salt and let stand for 1 - 1½ hours. Rinse the chicken in cold running water and pat dry, inside and out, with towelling.

2. Make the stuffing by combining and mixing well the rice, beef, parsley, bread crumbs, nuts, lemon and seasonings. Stuff the chicken and sew closed.

3. Place the chicken, stuffed side up, in a saucepan and cover with water. Bring to a boil and then lower the heat, cooking another ½ hour, partly covered. Remove the chicken from the broth and transfer to a baking dish. Pour a bit of oil over the chicken allowing drippings to sit in the casserole. Sprinkle the chicken with salt and pepper to taste. Place in hot oven until chicken is red-brown, basting occasionally with the oil. Serve hot.

Serves 4 - 6.

Chicken with Prune Stuffing

1 large roasting chicken, about 4½ lbs (2 kilo)
1½ lbs (675 gr) pitted prunes
2 tsp salt
1 tsp each sweet paprika and black pepper
½ tsp oregano

1. Place the prunes in a bowl and pour over boiling water to cover. Allow to stand 1 hour. With a slotted spoon remove the prunes and reserve the liquid.

2. Cut away unwanted fat from the chicken and wash the chicken thoroughly, inside and out. Pat dry with towelling and sprinkle cavity with 1 tsp salt. Sprinkle outside of chicken with remaining salt, pepper and paprika. Loosely stuff the cavity with the prunes, place in ovenproof casserole and roast in medium oven for 40 minutes, basting frequently with the liquid from the prunes. Add the remaining prunes and continue roasting until chicken is done (about 40-50 minutes). Serve hot.

Serves 6.

Chicken with Bread Stuffing

1 large roasting chicken, about 4½ lbs (2 kilo)
10 slices white bread, without crusts
3 medium onions, chopped
¼ cup each parsley and celery, finely chopped
2 eggs, lightly beaten
2 tsp salt
1 tsp each sugar, sweet paprika and black pepper
oil for frying
chicken stock for basting (page 77)
chicken fat for basting

1. Cut away unwanted fat and wash the chicken thoroughly, inside and out. Pat dry with towelling and sprinkle cavity with 1 tsp salt. Sprinkle outside of chicken with pepper and paprika.

2. Soak the bread in water for several minutes and then squeeze out by hand until nearly dry. Heat the oil in a skillet and in this sauté the onions until transparent. Transfer to a bowl the remaining ingredients, except the stock, and mix well until mixture is uniform.

3. Loosely stuff the cavity of the chicken, sewing closed if necessary. Transfer the chicken to an ovenproof casserole and roast in medium oven for 50 minutes, basting frequently with the stock. Cover the chicken with dots of chicken fat and continue roasting until chicken is done (about 30 minutes longer). Serve hot.

Serves 6.

Chicken with Mushrooms

1 medium-sized chicken
½ lb (225 gr) fresh mushrooms, sliced
¾ cup chicken stock (page 77)
½ cup bread crumbs
¾ cup sour cream
1 tblspn parsley, chopped
½ tsp each celery seed and salt
¼ tsp each dill weed and pepper
oil for frying

1. Cut the chicken into convenient serving pieces and dip the pieces in the bread crumbs, coating well. In a heavy skillet sauté the chicken in hot oil on both sides until golden. Add the parsley, celery seed, salt, dill weed and pepper and over this pour the chicken stock. Cover and on medium-low flame simmer 1 hour.

2. Remove the chicken from the skillet and place on serving platter. To the liquids add the sour cream. Heat through, adjust seasonings and pour over the chicken parts. Serve hot.

Serves 4.

Chicken Kiev

4 chicken breasts, skinned and boned
½ lb (225 gr) butter or margarine
8 tblspns parsley, chopped finely
3 eggs
½ cup dry bread crumbs
oil for deep frying
salt and pepper to taste

1. Allow the butter to soften at room temperature and then mix with the chopped parsley. Refrigerate until hard. Put the mixture inside the chicken breast and roll these up around the mixture. Close with one or two stitches.

2. Beat the eggs with 2 tblspns water. To the bread crumbs add the salt and pepper and mix. Dip the rolled chicken breasts first in the egg and then in the bread crumb mixture. Repeat until the breasts are well coated. Fry in deep

hot oil until well browned. Serve immediately. May be served with sour cream on the side.

Serves 4.

Poultry Stuffed Blintzes

Batter:

½ cup each flour, milk and water
2 eggs
1 tblspn butter

Filling:

½ lb (225 gr) chopped chicken breast
1 medium onion, chopped finely
2 tblspns chopped parsley
1 tsp salt
½ tsp pepper
¼ tsp coriander
oil for frying

Sauce:

½ chicken
2½ cups chicken stock (page 77)
¼ lb (115 gr) chopped almonds
1 tsp each salt, pepper, ground cinnamon
½ tsp sweet paprika

1. Sauté the onion in oil until golden. Add the ground beef and sauté until lightly browned. Remove from flame and add chopped parsley and seasonings for filling. Set aside.

2. Mix the batter ingredients together until the mixture obtains a smooth, somewhat runny texture. Heat a crepe pan and spread it with ½ tsp butter, making certain entire pan is coated. Put one tablespoon of the blintz mixture in the pan tilting and shaking to spread evenly. Leave for 30 seconds and turn. Cook second side another 30 seconds. (Blintzes should be lightly brown.) Transfer blintz to clean towel and repeat until all blintzes are done. Grease pan again only if absolutely necessary. Let cool.

3. Boil the chicken in water with the salt and pepper. When done remove from the liquid and cool. Remove skin and separate the chicken meat from the bones. Chop the meat coarsely. To this add the stock, ground nuts, paprika, cinnamon and salt and pepper to taste. Over a very low flame stirring constantly, heat until sauce thickens.
4. Fill the blintzes with the stuffing and roll up. Immediately cover with the sauce and serve hot.

Serves 4-6.

Giblet Fricasee

12 each chicken wings and gizzards
6 chicken livers, halved
2 onions, sliced
2 stalks celery, chopped
2 sprigs parsley, chopped
1 large green pepper, diced
2 tblspns chicken fat
1 tblspn flour
1 tsp dill weed
salt and pepper to taste
sweet paprika as needed

1. Pour boiling water over the gizzards, clean well and cut each into three sections. Place these in a saucepan with the wings, celery, parsley and dill. Add cold water to barely cover. Bring to a boil and then lower flame to simmer, covered, for 1 hour. Add the livers and simmer 15 minutes longer.
2. In a large skillet heat the fat and sauté the onions until translucent. Add green pepper and cook 10 minutes longer.
3. Remove the gizzards, wings and livers from the broth and add to the onion-pepper mixture. Season with salt and pepper. Sprinkle the mixture with the flour and, stirring gently, cook until all pieces are well coated. Add ½ cup of the broth and cook several minutes longer, stirring, while sauce thickens. Sprinkle with paprika and serve hot.

Note: Strain and reserve the broth in sealed container, refrigerated for later use as stock or soup.

Serves 6.

Grilled Chicken Livers

2 lbs (900 gr) chicken livers, halved
½ cup olive oil
4 tsp vinegar
3 cloves garlic, chopped
½ tsp each salt, pepper, cumin

1. Combine and mix well the oil, vinegar and seasonings. Pour over the chicken livers and allow to stand 3-4 hours, turning occasionally.
2. Over an open flame or in a hot broiler, grill the livers until well browned on the exterior. Serve hot.

Serves 4.

Roast Stuffed Goose

1 goose, about 6-8 lbs (2½-3 kilos)
6 large potatoes, peeled, boiled and well mashed
3 onions, grated
½ cup parsley, chopped finely
2 eggs, lightly beaten
1 tsp each caraway seed and black pepper
salt to taste

1. Rinse the goose under cold, running water and then pat dry with towelling. Combine the remaining ingredients and stuff the goose lightly. Sew closed and place, breast up, on a rack in an open roasting pan. Place in medium oven and roast 20-25 minutes per pound (40-45 minutes per kilo). After first five minutes in the oven prick the skin. Prick skin periodically after this and baste often using the juices in the pan. The goose will be done when the leg joints move easily. Serve hot.

Serves 6-8.

Roast Duckling with Apples

1 duckling, about 4 lbs (1¾ kilo)
6 large cooking apples
2 onions, chopped coarsely
1 tsp salt
¾ tsp black pepper

1. Rinse the duckling under cold, running water and then pat dry with towelling. Rub the duckling, inside and out with salt and pepper. Place in roasting pan, sprinkle inside and out with onions and surround by the apples (skinned, cored and quartered). Roast 1 ½ hours, occasionally basting the duckling and fruit with drippings.

Serves 4 - 6.

Beyond the Gefilte

WITHOUT JESUS there would be no Christianity; Buddhism is dependent upon the personage of Gautama Siddhartha; and without Mohammed there would be no Islam. But Judaism is different. Even without gefilte fish there would be Judaism.

As much as European Jews and their ancestors have become associated with the renowned gefilte, a careful study will reveal not a single mention of this delicacy in the Old Testament, the Talmud or the films of Mel Brooks. It is probably true that Jews have no other fish before the gefilte, but it is equally evident that quite a few other fish hold parallel places in the collective Jewish heart.

Long considered a luxuriant food, it has been traditional to celebrate the eve of the Sabbath by serving the finest fish one could find in the market. Despite the frequent economic hardships which most Eastern European Jews suffered, many families would only begin to consider themselves poor if they could not afford a fine fish dinner on this special night. It was also considered good form to welcome guests into one's home by serving an especially fine fish dinner. This was done not so much to impress the visitor with one's wealth, but as a sign of honour to him.

The love of Jews for fish became so well known that at least some portions of the general population came to believe that Jews ate fish in some secret, ritualistic manner that would increase their sexual potency and their financial abilities. As a result of this nonsense it was forbidden, during the Middle Ages, to sell fish to Jews. (I have suggested to Woody Allen a comedy-suspense-musical film based on this historical phenomenon but have not yet received a response to my letter.)

The only serious problem European Jews had with fish was in assuring their supply. While Mediterranean and North African Jews were sometimes fishermen by trade, the Jews of the shtetls of Russia, Poland and the Balkans were frequently landlocked and thus dependent for their supplies on local fishmongers. One week might find the market with an abundance of carp or perch, the next with buffalo fish or sea bass, and yet another with herrings or pike. This called for a bit of ingenuity in the kitchen, for frequently one would not know what fish was to grace the table until half an hour before it had to be prepared. Many of the recipes that developed in the Yiddish kitchen were therefore somewhat androgynous — nearly any fish could be used in nearly any recipe.

As, for example, gefilte fish could be made with carp and pike, pike and buffalo fish or any of these alone, it became traditional to have recipes not so much for specific dishes as for baked, broiled, or poached fish. The particular fish that happened to find its way into the recipe under use being simply that one fortunate or unfortunate enough to have found its way to market that day.

This is not, however, to imply a limitation on the number of recipes available. On Kiev's Street of the Crooked Cobbler were eighteen Jewish families. Between them they boasted over three hundred and fifty fish recipes. And that was before even starting to consider the correct way to prepare a gefilte.

D.R.

Baked Mackerel

2 lbs (900 gr) mackerel fillets
2 onions, sliced
2 potatoes, peeled and sliced thinly
1 large tomato, sliced thinly
2 stalks celery, chopped
3 tblspns butter
juice of 2 lemons
salt and pepper to taste
paprika as needed

1. In a greased casserole arrange half the vegetables. On these lay the fillets, sprinkle with salt, pepper and lemon juice and dot with the butter. Cover the fish with the remaining vegetables and sprinkle with paprika. Bake, covered, in medium oven until fish flakes easily with a fork (about 30 minutes). Serve hot.

Serves 4.

Poached Whitefish

1 large whitefish, about 3½ lbs (1½ kilo)
3 large onions, sliced
2 large carrots, sliced
2 stalks celery
3 tblspns parsley, finely chopped
2 tblspns sugar
2 tsp salt
½ tsp white pepper

1. In a large, fairly shallow pot place the vegetables, seasonings and 2½ cups water. Bring to a boil and let boil, covered, for 10 minutes.
2. Clean the fish, discarding head and tail and cut remainder into 1½-2" (4-5 cm) slices. Arrange the fish slices on the vegetables. Reduce to low flame, cover and simmer for 1 hour.
3. Remove the fish from the stock. Adjust stock seasoning, strain and pour ½ cup over the fish. (Remainder may be stored for later use if covered and refrigerated.) Serve hot.

Serves 4.

Deep Fried Fresh Water Fish

4 fresh water fish (e.g. trout), about 1 lb (450 gr) each
¼ lb (115 gr) butter
salt and pepper to taste
oil for deep frying

1. Clean the fish and dry well on a towel. Season to taste with salt and pepper.
2. Heat the oil for deep frying and fry the fish until nearly done. Remove from the oil and place in baking dish. Melt the butter and pour over the fish. Cover and place in hot oven until fish is done (should flake easily to the touch of a fork). Serve hot garnished with parsley and lemon wedges.

Serves 4.

Grilled Herring with Fennel

4 herrings about ½ lb (225 gr) each
3 tblspns butter
1 tsp fennel
½ tsp salt
juice of 1 large lemon
oil for basting

1. Clean fish well, cutting off heads and trimming tails. On each side cut three narrow slits. Mix the fennel and salt and insert in the cuts and in the body cavity.
2. In a low baking dish melt the butter. Add the lemon juice. Lay the fish in this mixture and turn once to coat both sides. Grill on open fire or under hot broiler for 4 - 5 minutes on each side. Baste once on each side with the oil and the drippings. Serve hot.

Serves 4.

Trout in Sour Cream

4 small trout, cleaned
1 ½ cups sour cream
2 onions, sliced
4 tblspns butter, melted
1 tblspn paprika
½ tsp each salt and pepper

1. Sprinkle both sides of the fish with salt and pepper and arrange in a greased baking dish. Over the fish lay the onion slices.
2. Mix the sour cream and paprika and pour over the fish. Place in a low oven and bake 45 minutes basting occasionally with the melted butter. Serve hot.

Serves 4.

Fillet of Sole with Almonds

1 lb (450 gr) fillets of sole
½ cup milk
¼ cup blanched shredded almonds
3 tblspns flour
butter for frying

1. Dip the fillets into the milk and then dust with the flour.
2. In a skillet melt enough butter to well cover the bottom and in this sauté the fillets, turning once. Remove the finished fillets to a serving platter and keep warm. Melt an additional 2-3 tblspns butter and in this lightly brown the almonds. Pour the almond and butter mixture over the fillets; garnish with lemon wedges and parsley. Serve hot.

Serves 3-4.

Baked Fish in White Sauce

1 whitefish, about 3½ lbs (1½ kilo)
1 cup milk
3 tblspns butter plus butter for basting
2 tblspns each chopped parsley and chives
1½ tblspns flour
1 tsp lemon juice
salt and pepper to taste

1. Clean and scale the fish and slit the skin in several places. Place in a well greased ovenproof casserole and rub generously, inside and out, with 1 tblspn butter. Place the fish in a low oven and bake, basting generously with additional butter as needed, until fish flakes easily to the touch of a fork (about 35-40 minutes).

2. Several minutes before the fish is done, in a large saucepan melt 2 tblspns butter and add, stirring constantly, the flour. Stir well until flour and butter are well blended and then continuing to stir constantly, slowly add the milk. After the mixture is well blended and has thickened, stir in the seasonings. Pour the sauce over the fish. Serve hot.

Serves 4-6.

Baked Whitefish with Sour Cream

1 whitefish, about 3½ lbs (1½ kilo)
2 cups sour cream
2 tblspns butter
1 tsp sweet paprika
1 tsp parsley, chopped finely

1. Split and remove the bones from the fish. Flatten the fish and rub inside and out with the butter and paprika. Place the fish in an ovenproof casserole dish and pour over the sour cream. Bake, covered, in medium oven until the fish flakes easily to the touch of a fork (about 45 minutes). Sprinkle with the parsley just before serving.

Serves 4.

Genetic Traits

Now these are the ordinances . . .
Exodus 21:1

FOR FIFTY centuries and for various reasons at various times, the world has been trying to figure out precisely what and who the Jews are. Ranging a gamut of definitions from that of the Torah Sages of Agudat Israel (about the holiest collection of men to which one may aspire to belonging if one is an orthodox Jew) to Adolph Hitler (one of the most unholy of men by any definition), there are two hundred and twenty-seven ways in which to determine precisely just who is and who is not a Jew. None of these definitions is correct! The only true way to determine Jewishness is through a series of nine traits, each of which is genetically determined and each of which relates directly or indirectly to food.

1. All Jews enjoy eating.
2. All Jewish men are convinced that all Jewish women enjoy cooking, but that no Jewish woman cooks as well as their own mothers.
3. All Jewish women do enjoy cooking and they too acknowledge that no other Jewish woman cooks as well as their own mothers.

4. All Jews most enjoy eating that food which has been prepared by their own mothers.
5. All Jews feel guilty about their mothers.
6. Because all Jews feel guilty about their mothers, they cannot enjoy eating the food which has been prepared by their mothers as much as is demanded by their genetic propensity.
7. Because this genetic drive is frustrated, all Jews are either over- or underweight and no Jew feels that his or her weight is ideal.
8. When Jews are not enjoying their food (that is to say, when they are feeling guilty, frustrated or both), they are either on diets or overeating. Diets, although they do not satisfy the stomach, are said to be good for the psyche. Overeating, which, although it is not particularly good for the figure, is an excellent palliative for the psyche.
9. Whether they over- or undereat, all Jews are therefore happy and unhappy, frustrated and content, up and down, elated and depressed, over- and underweight — all at the same moment.

Nobody has ever claimed that being Jewish was simple.

D.R.

Cucumber Salad

6 medium cucumbers
2 medium onions, sliced thinly
1 cup sour cream
1 tblspn salt
½ tblspn vinegar
1½ tsp sugar
1 tsp dill seed
½ tsp sweet paprika

1. Peel the cucumbers and slice thinly. Separate the onion slices into rings. Combine these in a serving bowl and sprinkle with the salt and allow to stand for 2 hours. Drain whatever liquid has accumulated from the mixture.
2. In a separate bowl put the sour cream and mix with the sugar and vinegar. Add remaining ingredients, except the paprika, mix and spoon over the salad, mixing gently. Sprinkle with paprika and serve at room temperature or slightly chilled.

Serves 4-6.

111

Cucumbers in Sour Cream

3 large cucumbers
½ cup sour cream
juice of 1 lemon
¾ tsp sugar
¼ tsp salt
pepper to taste

1. Slice cucumbers thin. Mix all remaining ingredients, pour over cucumbers and mix gently.

Serves 3-4.

Beet Salad

3 medium red beets
3 spring onions, finely chopped
2 tblspns olive oil
1 tblspn vinegar
1 tsp salt
½ tsp each pepper and cumin
juice of 2 lemons

1. Cook the beets in lightly salted water until soft. Peel and cut in thin slices.
2. Combine remaining ingredients and mix well. Pour over the beets, mixing gently. May be served warm or chilled. Garnish with green olives.

Serves 4-6.

Beet Salad in Sour Cream

1 lb (450 gr) beets
1 cup sour cream
3 tblspns chopped chives
½ tsp tarragon
salt and pepper to taste

1. In a saucepan with lightly salted water, boil the beets until tender. Remove from water, peel and cut into ½″ (1 cm) cubes.
2. To the sour cream add the spices and season with salt and pepper to taste. Mix with the beet cubes. Cover and refrigerate. Serve cold.

Serves 4-6.

Carrot Salad

1 lb (450 gr) small carrots
10 spring onions
4 tblspns olive oil
1 ½ tblspns vinegar
½ tblspn chopped parsley
½ tsp each dill weed, savory, salt and sugar
¼ tsp black pepper

1. Scrape carrots clean and grate using hand grater. Slice the onions finely. Place in serving bowl.
2. Beat the vinegar and oil together with the seasonings, except the parsley. Pour over the carrots and onions and toss thoroughly. Garnish with the parsley immediately before serving. Serve cold.

Serves 4-6.

Carrot Salad with Raisins

4 large carrots, grated
½ cup seedless raisins
⅓ cup orange juice
sugar to taste

1. In a bowl combine all of the ingredients, mixing well. Starting with 1 tsp sugar mix and taste, adjusting the amount of sugar to individual taste.

Serves 3-4.

Stuffed Tomatoes

4 large tomatoes
6 hard boiled eggs, diced finely
3 stalks celery, diced finely
1 medium onion, chopped coarsely
3 tblspns mayonnaise
1 tblspn sour cream
1 tsp prepared mustard
½ tsp each salt, pepper and dill seed
2-3 drops Tabasco (optional)

1. Cut off the top ¼ of the tomatoes. Remove the pulp and seeds.
2. Blend together, gently, the remaining ingredients and with this fill the tomatoes. Refrigerate, covered, until well chilled. Garnish with green olives.

Serves 4.

Cabbage Salad

1 medium head cabbage, shredded
½ cup vinegar
¼ cup oil
1½ tblspns prepared mustard
1 tsp sugar
½ tsp salt

1. Rinse and drain the cabbage thoroughly. Mix the mustard, sugar, salt and vinegar until smooth. Add to this the oil and ¼ cup water. Mix well and pour over the cabbage. Toss, cover and let stand ½ hour before serving. Toss again before serving.

Serves 4-6.

Red Cabbage Salad

1 medium head red cabbage, shredded
½ cup red wine vinegar
½ cup oil
1 tblspn sugar
1 tsp salt

114

1. In a large saucepan boil lightly salted water and in this immerse the shredded cabbage. Cook until water boils again. Drain the cabbage thoroughly.
2. Mix the vinegar, sugar and salt. Add the oil and ¾ cup water and blend together well. Pour the dressing over the cabbage and let stand 1 hour before serving. Toss again immediately before serving.

Serves 4-6.

Charosis

This delicacy is generally served at Passover. Always served in small quantities, it is a delicious taste treat when spread on a small piece of matzo.

1 large sour apple, peeled and cored
½ cup walnuts or pecans, very finely chopped
2 tblspns sweet red wine
1 tblspn sugar
¾ tsp cinnamon

1. Grate the apple finely and combine with remaining ingredients. Mix thoroughly.

Yields about 1 cup.

The Jewish Vegetarian

. . the cucumbers, and the melons, and the leeks, and the onions and the garlic . .
Numbers 11:5

MOST JEWS who become vegetarians do so neither for reasons of health or aesthetics. Simply stated, vegetarianism provides a simplified access to paradise.

It must be undertsood that for orthodox Jews, the laws of *kashrut* play an important role in daily life. In addition to ensuring, for example, that meats have been ritually slaughtered and prepared, one must also be certain that *fleishig* (meat) and *milchig* (dairy) products will not be consumed in the same meal. For the devout this involves maintaining two sets of dishes for daily use and an additional double set for Passover. Some even maintain fully separate kitchens for meat and dairy. It is not simple, and even the accidental transgressor finds him or herself with a certain measure of guilt, a somewhat queasy stomach and at least three steps closer to *gehenna* (hell). Considering that Talmudic lore goes to great trouble to spell out in excruciating detail the location, size and divisions of *gehenna* where wicked souls burn and are otherwise made to suffer, this is not precisely an invitation that beckons.

Vegetarianism simplifies all of this. By eating only foods that are either dairy or *parve* (not considered either meat or dairy) a great many accidental failings and temptations may be avoided. This may indeed be the lazy person's access to heaven but there are other advantages as well. While avoiding pitfalls it leaves the individual a fair amount of choice. *Parve* foods, for example, include all of the fruits, cereals and vegetables as well as (pardon the expression) the meat of the fishes. This means that one who has gone the vegetarian route need not be concerned between the choice of butter or margarine in preparing foods and sauces. In addition to eliminating the need for double sets of dishes it is always less expensive to eat dairy and *parve* products. Finally, for those who so desire, it is a great deal easier to raise and prepare one's own vegetables than meats. Carrots don't eat as much, don't smell as badly and do not raise quite as many objections on the part of one's neighbours as do cows, lambs or chickens. Particularly for the city dweller this is an advantage not to be overlooked.

Then, too, it is always better to deal with vegetable store owners than with butchers. It is difficult enough to work up a genuine sense of affection for a man with a cleaver in his hand and most butchers act as if they are doing their clients a favour by yielding up a decent cut of beef. At least greengrocers are polite.

There is one type of Jewish vegetarian that I have always found a bit suspicious. These are those men and women who have stretched the rules of the game just enough to have decided that chicken, too, is allowable in their vegetarian diet. With such souls one cannot help but wonder whether they occasionally pop into their local hamburger emporium for a well rationalized but not truly reasonable escape. Anyone who has to sneak out for a hamburger cannot be completely above suspicion.

Then there was my *Buba* (grandmother). A devoted vegetarian, Buba never let us hear the end of the sins of our own carnivorous ways. She did, however, have the odd habit of tasting absolutely everything that had been prepared for the family's consumption. Something of a middle-class royal taster, Buba probably consumed, at least in proportion to her eighty-pound frame, as much meat as did any of the physically larger family members.

All of that was acceptable. What did rankle a bit was that from the age of 90 onwards, Buba spent as many hours as possible telling as many people as possible that her longevity was entirely due to her vegetarian habits. If memory serves, her last repast was taken while sampling a pot roast of beef. Considering that the beef was cooking in green beans and carrots that probably justified it all for Buba.

D.L.

Glazed Carrots in Honey

1 ½ lbs (675 gr) carrots, scraped and sliced
3 tblspns butter
1 tblspn cornflour
2 ½ tsp honey
1 ½ tsp sugar

1. In a saucepan place the carrots and pour over lightly salted boiling water to cover. Cook until partially tender and remove from flame. Reserve ½ cup of the liquid and drain the carrots.
2. Mix the cornflour with the liquid and combine with the honey and sugar.
3. In a skillet melt the butter, add the carrots and stir in the honey mixture. Continue stirring until carrots are well coated. Cook over low flame until carrots are tender and glazed (about 5 - 7 minutes).

Serves 6.

Tzimmis

This carrot and prune dish is a Passover speciality but is delightful enough to be served at any time during the year. One will be well advised to know that "making a tzimmis" has a double meaning. On the one hand it refers to the dish and on the other to making "much ado about nothing".

2 lbs (900 gr) carrots, sliced thinly
1 cup each pitted prunes and honey
½ cup seedless raisins
6 tblspns butter
4 tblspns matzo meal flour
2 tblspns lemon juice
½ tsp each salt, nutmeg and cinnamon
¼ tsp ground cloves

1. Place the carrots in a saucepan and barely cover with water. Bring to a boil, reduce heat, add prunes, raisins and simmer, uncovered, until tender. Add the honey, salt and lemon juice. Cover and on very low flame, simmer 20 minutes longer.

2. In a skillet melt the butter and add to this the matzo meal, nutmeg and cloves, mixing to a thick paste. Add this to the carrot mixture and stir well until thickened. Brown quickly under a broiler immediately before serving and then sprinkle gently with the cinnamon. Serve hot.

Serves 8-10.

Sweet and Sour Beets

1 lb (450 gr) beets, peeled
½ lb (225 gr) carrots, sliced
2 tblspns each vinegar and soya sauce
2 tblspns oil

1. Place beets and carrots in a saucepan and cover with water. Cook on low flame for 1½ hours. Add the remaining ingredients and cook ½ hour longer. Serve hot.

Serves 4-6.

Glazed Beets

1 lb (450 gr) beets, peeled
¼ cup sugar
1 tblspn each lemon juice and oil
1½ tsp potato starch
½ tsp salt
¼ tsp pepper

1. In a saucepan with water to cover cook the beets until tender. Remove the beets from the liquid, reserving ½ cup for glaze. Slice the beets thinly.
2. Combine the reserved liquid, sugar, salt, pepper, salad oil and lemon juice in saucepan. Bring to a boil. Combine the potato starch with 1 tblspn cold water and add this to the boiling liquid, stirring constantly for 2-3 minutes. Add the sliced beets and cook, stirring gently, for 2 minutes longer. Serve hot.

Serves 4.

Red Cabbage and Apples

1 large red cabbage, cored and shredded
6 sour cooking apples, peeled, cored and sliced
4 tblspns butter
1 small onion, chopped
1 tblspn sugar
1 tsp each caraway seeds, paprika, salt

1. Place the shredded cabbage in a deep bowl and pour over boiling water to cover. Let stand 10 minutes and drain.
2. In a large skillet melt the butter and sauté the onions until golden brown. Add cabbage and remaining ingredients to the skillet. Add ¼ cup water, cover, and cook over low flame until cabbage is soft (about 1 hour). Add water if necessary. Serve hot.

Serves 6.

Red Cabbage in Wine

2 lbs (900 gr) red cabbage, cored and finely shredded
2 large cooking apples, peeled, cored and chopped
1 large onion, sliced thinly
½ cup dry red wine
¼ cup cider vinegar
3 tblspns each brown sugar and butter
3 whole cloves
1 tsp salt
½ tsp caraway seeds

1. In a large saucepan melt the butter and sauté the onions until golden brown. Add remaining ingredients, stir well and bring to a boil. Lower flame and simmer, uncovered, for ½ hour, stirring occasionally. Serve hot.

Serves 6-8.

Candied Sweet Potatoes

4 large sweet potatoes
1 cup brown sugar
1 tsp lemon rind, grated finely
salt and pepper to taste
butter as required
pinch ginger

1. In a saucepan with lightly salted boiling water cook the sweet potatoes about ½ hour or until just tender. Peel and slice the potatoes and arrange these in a lightly greased casserole dish. Season with salt and pepper and then sprinkle with the brown sugar, lemon rind and ginger. Dot the potato slices with butter and bake, uncovered, in medium oven for 20 - 25 minutes. Serve hot.

Serves 4 - 6.

Potatoes and Onions in Sour Cream

1 lb (450 gr) potatoes, peeled and sliced thin
2 medium onions, chopped
1 cup sour cream
6 tblspns butter
salt and pepper to taste

1. Melt 2 tblspns of the butter in a large skillet and in this sauté the onions until golden brown. With a slotted spoon remove the onions and set aside. Melt the remaining butter and cook the potatoes, covered, until tender.
2. Add the onions and salt and pepper and cook over low flame for 5 minutes longer. Slowly stir in the sour cream and heat until warm throughout. Serve hot.

Serves 4.

Mushrooms in Sour Cream

1 lb (450 gr) mushroom caps, whole
1 medium onion, chopped
1 cup sour cream
3 tblspns butter
2 tsp flour
salt and pepper to taste
paprika as required

1. In a skillet heat the butter and in this sauté the mushroom caps and onion until onions are translucent. Season with salt and pepper, mix in the flour and cook, covered, on low flame for 5 minutes. Remove from heat and allow

to cool for 5 minutes. Stir in the sour cream and heat, on very low flame until warm through. Sprinkle over with paprika and serve hot.

Serves 4.

Cauliflower with Bechamel Sauce

1 medium head cauliflower
1½ cups Bechamel sauce (page 53)
8 tblspns grated Parmesan cheese
1 tsp ground nutmeg
1 tsp salt
pinch cinnamon

1. Clean the cauliflower and separate into flowerettes. Cook in salted water until nearly soft. Drain and place in a shallow casserole.
2. Pour the Bechamel sauce over the cauliflower. Season with the grated nutmeg and cinnamon. Sprinkle the grated cheese on top of the mixture and cook in hot oven until dish is heated through and brown on top.

Serves 4.

Stuffed Tomatoes

4 large tomatoes
¾ cup brown rice, uncooked
6 tblspns olive oil
2 cloves garlic, finely chopped
2 tsp chopped parsley
2 tsp butter
1 tsp each sweet basil and black pepper
salt to taste

1. Cut tomatoes horizontally about ⅓ from the top. Set aside the cut-off portions. Scoop out the pulp and strain, reserving the liquids. Rub the inside of each tomato shell with a drop of oil and pinch of salt.
2. Mix 3 tblspns oil, rice, juice from tomatoes, salt, pepper, basil, parsley and garlic. With this mixture fill the tomato shells. On top of the mixture place ½ tsp butter. Cover each tomato with the pieces in reserve. Place tomatoes in

greased baking dish and pour the remaining oil over the tops. Bake in medium oven until rice is soft (about ½ hour). Serve hot.

Serves 4.

Stuffed Peppers

4 large green peppers
1½ cups cottage cheese
½ cup each spring onions and parsley, both chopped
2 eggs, well beaten
½ tsp salt

1. Slice off tops of peppers and remove seeds and pith. Place the peppers in saucepan and cover with cold water. Bring to a boil and boil 4-5 minutes. Drain.
2. Combine the remaining ingredients and mix well. Stuff peppers with the mixture. Arrange the peppers in a shallow baking dish with water to cover bottom of dish. Bake, in medium oven, until peppers are tender (25-35 minutes). Serve hot.

Serves 4.

Kugels, Kashe and Tsuris

. . . thou shalt eat and be satisfied.
Deuteronomy 8:10

IT IS FULLY possible that without the Yiddish language, Jewish food would not taste quite the same. *Kugel*, literally translated, means pudding, but even the most respectable pudding would not dare compare itself with even the most modest of kugels. *Kashe* are buckwheat groats, but when kashe has been lovingly prepared in the Yiddish kitchen it so far surpasses any of the grains known to humankind that referring to it by its English name is an insult, pure and simple.

As the taste of foods is enhanced by the language, so is the very flavour of life. This may then be the place for a modified lexicon of a few Yiddish words and phrases that have not yet been touched upon in this litle book. Considering that Yiddish, like Hebrew, is written backwards (that is to say, from right to left) we will waive the usual lexiconic requirement of alphabetization. As to categories, those fall entirely to the imagination, for as rich as the language may be, linguistic logic and the rules of grammar simply do not fully apply to Yiddish.

Jews particularly enjoy using terms that denote the traits and qualities of people. Some negative descriptors will serve as well as any for our jumping off point.

klutz: (noun) — a person who is far more than clumsy, the klutz manages to be simultaneously maladroit, inept and gauche. The klutz frequently manages to trip on his or her own shoelaces, falls over furniture, and manages to drip mustard onto his or her lap with a regularity amazing enough to confound the laws of probability. The qualities of being a klutz may be genetically inherited. Klutzes are not unloved as they are usually the victims of their own misdeeds.

shlemeil: (noun) — all shlemeils are klutzes but shlemeils are rarely loved because the victims of their action are generally innocent bystanders. The true shlemeil is that waiter who invariably spills soup on his clients.

shlemazel: (noun) — these are the poor souls who are the victims of shlemeils. In a sense it is correct to state that a shlemazel is the shlemeil's shlemeil — they are the ones always having the soup dumped on them. A term frequently tinged with just a bit of pity.

shlumper: (noun) — a lost soul, not in the metaphysical sense but in the way of physical appearance. The shlumper always wears mismatched socks, a sweater two or more sizes too large, a shirt that is never quite clean, and trousers that look as if they were last pressed a year or more ago. Although shlumpers try hard to make good impressions they are doomed in their attempts as they have an irresistable attraction to mud puddles, dust, dandruff and whatever the dogs have left lying in the street.

shlep: (verb or noun) — literally means to haul. Jewish waiters, for example, do not walk from place to place — they shlep. Those who shlep often enough become known by the word.

shmendrick: (noun) — someone who should have known better. A woman who thinks she can reform the ways of a shlumper becomes a shmendrick for not having realized that shlumperism is incurable.

nudnik: (noun) — a pest, specifically of the human variety, the nudnik drives everyone quite mad with his or her activities. Always present and always in the way, the nudnik is often tolerated but rarely loved.

tsuris: (adj) — a wide assortment of problems, tsuris is what nudniks have and are only too willing to share with others.

shnorer: (noun) — a particular type of nudnik, the shnorer is basically a freeloader. The shnorer's problem is that although he or she does not have whatever you do, they generally manage to get at least some of it at your expense. Shnorers rarely pay for the drinks.

125

kvetch: (noun) — another special variety of nudnik, the kvetch thrives on complaining. For the kvetch nothing ever goes right, especially if it was arranged by someone else. Everything is too hot, too cold, too much or too little. The kvetch can never be satisfied. One is well advised not to try too hard.

yenta: (noun, always feminine) — the yenta is the kvetch *par excellence*. Although she will rarely tell you precisely what is wrong she thrives on her ability to complain about absolutely anything, to anyone and at any time. A completely reliable sub-species.

oy veyes mei: (uncategorizable) — the favourite expression of kvetches in general and yentas in particular, this is something akin to the Old English "woe is me", the French "merde" and the night howl of the wild coyote in heat. If one wants to complain bitterly there is no better expression.

Lest it be thought that Yiddish is a language particularly suited to kvetching, it should be known too that the jargon abounds with homilies devoted to terms of endearment and affection.

bubele: (noun or adj) — literally "sweetheart" this term is reserved for use by parents in describing their very young children or by older parents when they want to remind their by now middle-aged offspring of their subjectivity. A wonderful term to use with adults when desiring to instill feelings of guilt.

motek: (noun or adj) — something akin to the American "cutey-pie". Acceptable when used to describe either infants or lovers. Strangers may react with hostility.

tsutsik: (noun) — literally "small one" but used as a term of endearment and even as an acceptable nickname for intimate friends. Also may be used in provoking a fight when put in the sarcastic mode.

shane punim: (adj or noun) — literally "pretty face" but more to describe a person of gentle and loving personality. Definitely not to be used when addressing gangsters or stockbrokers.

The language also boasts a collection of words and phrases that, because they fit into no special category, are applicable to absolutely anything.

nu: (exclamation, question, declarative sentence or declaration of war) — literally means "so" but what it *really* means is a matter of pronunciation, accompanying hand gestures and specific context. "Nu? It's not good enough for you?" is a question that dare not be answered in the negative. "Nu? You're ready yet or not?" defies an answer that will satisfy the questioner. On its own "Nu!!!" may, depending on many factors, express disgust, impatience, anger, sarcasm or simple curiosity. For the uninitiated, this term is to be used with caution.

kvell: (verb) — to kvell is to express pleasure in a gentle manner. Cats kvell when they purr and people do so in similar fashions. Men and women are especially prone to kvelling when they want something from you.

ah, machaya: (uncategorizable) — a phrase that expresses deep momentary satisfaction. Especially appropriate when taking off shoes that have been too tight, tasting a good plate of cholent, or on the first realization that the object of one's lust is responding positively.

bissele: (adj) — a little bit. A bissele gefilte fish, a bissele herring and just a bissele bread in between meals makes for a wonderful snack.

shnippele: (adj) — an even littler bit. When the food in the pots smells especially tempting the wise guest will convince the chef to let them sample just a shnippele of this and a shnippele of that.

On that gastronomic note, on to the kugels and kashe.

D.L.

Noodle Kugel — 1st version

½ lb (225 gr) broad noodles
¾ cup raisins
5 tblspns sugar
3 tblspns butter
2 eggs, beaten
¾ tsp cinnamon
½ tsp salt

1. Put noodles in boiling, salted water and boil for 10 minutes. Drain and rinse quickly with cold water. Add the eggs, sugar, cinnamon, butter and raisins and pour the mixture into a round casserole so that the mixture will be between 1½-2" (4-5 cm) high. Bake in medium oven for ½ hour. Serve hot or cold.

Serves 4-6.

Noodle Kugel — 2nd version

½ lb (225 gr) broad noodles
½ cup each sour cream and cottage cheese
5 tblspns sugar
3 tblspns butter
2 eggs, beaten
½ tsp each salt and cinnamon

1. Put noodles in boiling, salted water and cook for 10 minutes. Drain and rinse quickly with cold water. Add the remaining ingredients and stir well. Pour the mixture into a round casserole so that the mixture will be between 1½-2″ (4-5 cm) high. Bake in medium oven for ½ hour. Serve hot or cold.

Serves 4-6.

Noodle Kugel with Cheese and Raisins

1 lb (450 gr) broad noodles
2 cups cottage cheese
1 cup seedless raisins
½ cup cream cheese
¼ cup sugar
6 tblspns unsalted butter
4 eggs, separated
½ tsp cinnamon
¼ tsp salt

1. Cook noodles until almost tender. Drain, rinse and place in large mixing bowl. Add the butter and mix until melted.
2. Soften the cream cheese by allowing to stand at room temperature several hours and breaking up with a fork. Beat the egg yolks with the sugar, cinnamon and salt. Add the cottage and cream cheese and mix in the raisins. After the mixture is well blended, add and mix in the noodles.
3. Beat the egg whites until stiff and fold into the noodle mixture. Pour the mixture into a well greased baking dish and bake in a medium oven for 30 minutes. Raise heat to very high and bake an additional 10 minutes. Kugel is finished when the crust is golden brown.

Serves 6-8.

Noodle Kugel with Cheese and Apples

1 lb (450 gr) broad noodles
1 ½ cups cottage cheese
½ cup cream cheese
1 cup sour cream
4 green apples, peeled, cored and diced
4 eggs, lightly beaten
6 tblspns butter

1. Cook noodles until almost tender. Drain, rinse quickly and place in large mixing bowl. Add the butter and mix until melted.
2. Soften the cream cheese by allowing to stand at room temperature several hours and breaking up with a fork. Add the cream cheese and remaining ingredients to the noodles and mix thoroughly. Pour the mixture into a well greased baking dish and bake in medium oven for 1 hour, or until crust is golden brown.

Serves 6-8.

Potato Kugel — 1

8 large potatoes, peeled and quartered
4 medium onions, chopped coarsely
½ cup butter
2 eggs, lightly beaten
3 tblspns flour
¾ tsp baking powder
salt and pepper to taste
pinch ground nutmeg

1. Place potatoes in large saucepan and cover with lightly salted water. Cook, covered, until soft. Drain and mash thoroughly.
2. In a skillet melt the butter and in this sauté the onions until golden brown. Pour the onions and the melted butter over the mashed potatoes, add all other ingredients and mix thoroughly. Place this in a greased casserole dish and bake in moderately hot oven until crust is golden (40-50 minutes).

Serves 6-8.

Potato Kugel — 2

8 medium potatoes
3 eggs, separated
1 large onion, chopped finely
¼ cup Gruyere or Emmenthal cheese, grated
salt and pepper to taste
oil for frying

1. Boil the potatoes in salted water until very tender. Drain and mash thoroughly.
2. In a skillet heat the oil and in this sauté the onions until golden brown. Add the onions and beaten egg yolks to the potato purée. Beat the egg whites stiff, then fold into the mixture. Place in a greased baking dish, sprinkle with the cheese and bake in moderate oven until the kugel is lightly browned on top (about 30 minutes).

Serves 6-8.

Kashe with Noodles and Onions

Whether this particular dish is referred to as *Kashe Varnishkis, Kashe Vere-nishkes* or simply as *Verenishkes* depends on whether one is a Litvak or a Galiziano. Such feuds, however, are best left to grandparents. The dish, no matter how spelled or pronounced, is delicious.

1 cup kashe (buckwheat groats)
1 cup bow-tie noodles
¼ chicken fat
4 medium onions, diced
1 egg, lightly beaten
1 beef bouillon cube
1 tsp salt

1. In a hot skillet brown the kashe over a high flame until well toasted, stirring constantly for about 3-4 minutes. Stir in the beaten egg and cook 5 minutes, stirring rapidly and constantly so that each grain of kashe is coated and to avoid having the eggs set. Add 1 cup boiling water, the bouillon cube and salt, stirring until the bouillon is dissolved. Cook, covered, on medium flame for 10 minutes.

2. In a separate skillet melt the chicken fat and in this sauté the onions until golden brown.

3. In lightly salted water cook the noodles until tender. Drain and rinse quickly.

4. Transfer the kashe and the remaining liquid to a large saucepan and to this add the onions in the fat. Stir well, add ½ cup boiling water and cook over medium flame, covered, until the liquid is reduced but the kashe is still moist. Lower flame, add the noodles, stir well and cook, uncovered, 3 - 4 minutes longer. Serve hot.

Serves 4 - 6.

Kashe and Almonds

1 cup kashe
½ cup almonds, chopped coarsely
4 tblspns chicken fat
1 large onion, chopped coarsely

1. In a large skillet melt 2 tblspns of the chicken fat and in this sauté the onions until golden. With a slotted spoon remove the onions and reserve. Melt the remaining fat and in this brown the kashe, stirring continuously until each grain is coated. Add to this 3½ cups boiling water, cover and cook on medium flame for 15 minutes. Add the onions and almonds to the mixture, stir well, re-cover and bake in medium oven for 1 hour.

Serves 4.

No More Mannah for the Jews

And the house of Israel called the bread thereof Mannah; and it was like coriander seed, white; and the taste of it was like wafers made with honey.
Exodus 16:31

THERE ARE TWO points of view concerning *mannah*. The first is that this unlimited supply of tasty bread was really quite a good deal. For forty years, as the children of Israel wandered through the Sinai they could sleep comfortably, for each morning, shortly after dawn, they would be graced with as much of this delicacy as they consume in the day. Delivered directly from the heavens, one had to do no more than gather his or her share, eat as much as they liked and then look forward to the next day's crop. To make life even better, each night saw the camps visited by large numbers of quail and it was from these particularly cooperative birds that the people took their daily portion of meat.

The second point of view is a bit more caustic. One speculates that forty years of mannah and quail proved a heckuva monotonous diet. One need only consider the limitation of the menus available: mannah with quail, quail with mannah, mannah without quail and quail without mannah. And that, with the possible exception of quail fritters, quail soup and quail stuffed with mannah exhausts the possibilities.

For better or for worse, the recipe for mannah has long been misplaced and quail (possibly because we ate so many in the Sinai) has become a rare and expensive dish. Since that time, with three exceptions, Jews have adopted the breads served in the areas where they settled. The only truly "Jewish breads" are challah, bagels and matzo.

Challah, prepared especially for the Sabbath and holidays, is a rich, egg-based white bread possessed of a delicate bouquet and a taste and texture that sits well on the palate. Generally braided but sometimes served in loaf form, the ideal challah is well browned on the exterior and has a fluffy, deep yellow interior. An excellent accompaniment to a meal, challah also serves well for sandwiches, but its main joy may be given when served with a light coating of honey and butter.

Bagels are anything but delicate. Heavy enough to make excellent weapons but just a bit too small to make good frisbees, the bagel seems to have been designed especially to grace itself with a slice of lox, a bit of cream cheese or a modicum of butter. One of the main advantages to bagels is that with or without anything spread on or in them, they make the ideal bread for dunking in coffee or tea. And even a two-week-old bagel, reheated in the oven or under a broiler, is magnificent.

As to matzo there is little one can say. The unleavened bread served during the week of the Passover celebration, matzo is prized by all Jews, including this writer. Just why this is true is anyone's guess, for matzo in and of itself tastes something akin to a week-old newspaper or a well-used cardboard container. There is a trick, however, that turns matzo (at any time of the year) into a treat. It all depends on what you put on or do to the matzo.

Spread with butter and sprinkled with a bit of salt, matzo is a delicacy beyond comparison. When broken and mixed with eggs and seasonings and made into *matzo brei* (fried matzo) one is provided with a superb breakfast or brunch. Matzo is also tasty and serves as the basis for many sandwiches. In addition to good taste there is the positive challenge of making it through the sandwich before it crumbles to bits in one's hands. There was even a time when families prepared something which, for lack of a better name, was entitled "soggy matzo". Perhaps that recipe, along with that for mannah, remains best lost to the ages.

D.G.

Challah

The very special bread for the Sabbath but delicious on any occasion.

4 ½ cups flour
½ oz (15 gr) active dry yeast
2 eggs
2 egg yolks, beaten
2 tblspns each oil and sugar
2 tblspns poppy seeds
1 tblspn salt

1. Combine the yeast and sugar with ¼ cup warm water and set aside, uncovered, for 5-10 minutes.
2. Sift into a large mixing bowl 4 cups of the flour and the salt. With your hands, make a well in the centre of the flour-salt mixture and drop into this the oil, whole eggs and 1¼ cups warm water. Mix, working the liquids into the flour. When well mixed knead on a floured board until the dough is smooth. If too runny make the dough stiffer by adding flour until the mixture is elastic in nature.
3. Place the dough in a large bowl, brush the top with oil, cover with a towel and let stand to rise in a warm place for 1 hour.
4. Punch the dough down, cover and let rise again until doubled in size.
5. Divide the dough into three equal parts and, with floured hands, roll each piece into a strip, ensuring that each piece is the same length. Braid the strips and place them on a greased cookie sheet. Cover and let rise again until double in size. Brush the egg yolk over the top and sprinkle with the poppy seeds. Bake in moderately hot oven until well browned (about 40-50 minutes).

Yields 1 large or 2 small loaves.

Bagels

There are three things with which the Western world associates Jews: chicken soup, gefilte fish and bagels. These delectable rolls have come to a place of importance in the American Sunday breakfast for families Jewish or not; they are renowned in England and France for brunches; and in Eastern Europe they have become a dietary staple. In Israel, surprisingly, they are practically unknown, only recently having been introduced to supermarkets.

Bagels are remarkably versatile rolls. With a bit of butter they are magnificent for dunking in coffee; they are superb for small sandwiches; and nothing at all replaces the bagel for the very late night snack. It may (or it may not) have been Omar Khayyam who commented: "A bagel, a slice of lox and thou . . . "

4 cups flour
1 cup scalded milk
¼ cup butter
1 envelope dry active yeast
1 ½ tblspns sugar
1 tsp salt
1 egg, separated

1. Dissolve the yeast in ¼ cup lukewarm water, mix and let stand for 5-6 minutes.

2. Into a large mixing bowl pour the scalded milk and blend in the butter, sugar and salt. Stir in the yeast and to the mixture sift the flour. Beat the egg white stiff and fold gently into the mixture. Mix the dough well, cover the bowl with a towel and let stand 10 minutes.

3. On a well-floured board knead the dough for 5 minutes. Shape into a ball, cover with a damp cloth and let rise in a warm place until the volume doubles. Punch the dough down and divide into small balls. By hand roll each ball into tube-like shapes about 8″ (20 cm) long, and about the width of a thick finger. Connect the ends well, and let stand 10-15 minutes.

4. In a large saucepan filled ¾ with water, bring the water to a rapid boil. Reduce flame so that water is barely boiling and in this carefully drop the bagels, one at a time. Cook bagels 1 minute on each side. Remove to towelling.

5. Place the bagels on a well-greased cookie sheet. Beat the egg yolk with 1 tsp cold water and brush the tops of the bagels. Sprinkle each bagel with coarse salt (optional but delicious) and bake, in medium-hot oven until brown (about 45 minutes).

Yields about 24 bagels.

Pretzels

4 ½ cups flour
2 egg yolks
1 cake compressed yeast
½ tsp sugar
coarse salt as required

1. Combine 1¼ cups tepid water, the yeast and sugar and allow to stand at room temperature for 1½ hours. Into a large bowl with the flour pour this mixture and knead well for 5 - 7 minutes. Cover and allow the dough to rise until double in bulk. Form the dough into sticks about ¼" (½ cm) in diameter and about 6" (15 cm) long, and place these on a well-greased cookie sheet.
2. Combine and beat well the egg yolks with 5 tblspns water. With a brush, coat the pretzels with this mixture and then sprinkle generously with coarse salt. Allow the pretzels to rise until nearly doubled in diameter and then bake in a very hot oven for 10 minutes. Allow to cool completely before storing in a dry bread container.

Yields about 30 pretzels.

Pumpkin Bread

3 ½ cups flour
3 cups sugar
2 cups fresh pumpkin
1 cup corn oil
4 eggs
2 tsp baking soda
1 ¾ tsp cinnamon
1 ½ tsp each salt and nutmeg

1. To the eggs add 1 tsp water and beat well. Add the pumpkin, oil and ¾ cup water and blend well using blender or food processor. Sift the flour and mix into this the remaining ingredients. Sift this mixture into the pumpkin and mix well.
2. Grease two medium-sized loaf pans and sprinkle with flour. Pour in the batter and bake, in medium oven, for about 45 - 50 minutes. The breads will be done when the loaves have separated slightly from the pan and a knife blade inserted in the centre comes out clean.

Yields 2 loaves.

136

Quoth the Maven, Nevermore

NOT EVERYONE has to be a connoisseur. The French, in wise acknowledgement of this, give due credit to the *amateur*, the lover for example of wines or cheeses. The amateur finds life a bit easier than does the connoisseur, for while one must be a connoisseur of cuisine in general, it is possible to have full status as an amateur within a specific area of gastronomic endeavour. So it is, too, with the Jews, for as the French have their amateurs, so we have our *mavens*.

The only significant difference between the French and Jewish systems is that mavens must be truly dedicated specialists. There are, for example, herring mavens, borscht mavens and dessert mavens. While there is nothing to prevent one from being a maven in more than a single culinary realm, it does require a fair commitment to varying culinary specialties.

Of all the group, the dessert mavens may be the most adept, for most of the members of this devoted sect work diligently at involvement with the entire repertoire of desserts. This is no simple chore as the Yiddish kitchen offers a broad selection ranging from dessert blintzes to fruit compotes and from cakes to puddings. Being a dessert maven is enough to try the cholesterol count of any devotee.

True mavens, possibly because they have dedicated a major portion of their waking hours to their culinary adventures, enjoy seeking out others of their kind. When together it is logical that the two major topics under consideration are the quality of the desserts they have recently (or of old) sampled and the diets they invariably propose to start in the near future. The dessert maven, for good reason, is always promising to go on a diet. Yiddish desserts, with the exception of several simple but excellent fruit dishes, fall into three broad categories: very fattening, outrageously fattening and abominably fattening. The wise man or woman with a slow metabolism will do well to turn their mavenish desires to herring or to borscht, for dessert mavens do tend to overweight. It is obvious, however, that dieting and the love of desserts do not walk hand in hand.

A frequent chuckle may be obtained in one of the many New York, Paris or Tel Aviv eateries where a group of mavens have just worked their way through chocolate-filled blintzes, rice pudding and a baked apple topped with whipped cream, and are currently sitting at leisure over a cup of tea (without sugar) and discussing the need to give up the tea. Everyone credits the maven with love. Few credit them with moderation.

D.G.

Rice Pudding

1 cup uncooked rice
1½ quarts (1½ litres) milk
½ cup seedless raisins
½ cup sugar
½ tsp grated nutmeg
½ tsp vanilla extract
pinch salt
cinnamon to sprinkle

1. Soak raisins in water to cover for 1 - 1½ hours.
2. In a greased 2 quart (2 litre) casserole combine the rice, milk, sugar and salt. Bake, uncovered, in slow oven 1½ hours, stirring every 20 minutes.
3. Drain raisins and combine with the nutmeg and vanilla. Remove the rice mixture from the oven and stir in the raisins. Return to oven and bake additional ½ hour. Serve hot or cold. Immediately before serving sprinkle lightly with cinnamon.

Serves 6-8.

Chocolate Stuffed Blintzes

½ lb (225 gr) flour
6 eggs
⅓ cup oil
½ cup orange juice
½ cup high quality cocoa
4 oz (110 gr) butter plus butter for frying
1½ tblspns high quality brandy
1 tsp instant coffee
pinch salt
2½ tsp sugar

1. In a bowl put the oil, ½ cup water, pinch salt and ½ tsp sugar. Add 4 eggs and mix thoroughly. Into this slowly sift the flour, adding enough water until the mixture is even and somewhat runny.
2. Heat a crepe pan and melt in ½ tsp butter. Put spoonfuls of the batter into the pan tilting and shaking the pan to distribute the mixture evenly. Fry crepes quickly on both sides until the mixture has been used, setting crepes aside on clean towel. Grease the pan again only if absolutely necessary.
3. Into a saucepan put the cocoa, remaining sugar, instant coffee and brandy. Mix well. Add the remaining eggs and beat together. Add the orange juice and place the mixture over a medium flame, stirring constantly until a boil is reached. Lower the flame and cook 1 minute longer, stirring constantly.
4. Remove from the heat and add the butter. Stir well until the butter is completely dissolved and spread evenly throughout the mixture. Cool for at least 30 minutes. Fill the crepes with the cream and roll up. May be served with sweetened whipped cream.

Serves 6.

Marzipan Candy

2 cups sugar
2 cups blanched almonds, very finely ground
1½ tblspns lemon juice
2 egg whites, beaten stiffly

1. In a heavy saucepan on medium flame, heat the sugar and 1¼ cups water.

Stir constantly and when mixture begins to bubble at the edges add several drops of lemon juice. Continue heating and stirring until the mixture attains a syrup-like consistency. Lower flame, add the ground almonds and continue stirring until the mixture forms a ball the consistency of soft dough. Stir in the remaining lemon juice and when blended well, remove from heat.

2. Fold the stiff egg whites into the dough. Allow to cool, stirring occasionally, for 15-20 minutes and then roll out the dough to about ¾" (2 cm) thickness. Cut the marzipan into cookie-like shapes. Serve fresh or store in sealed containers.

Yields 30-36 candies.

Custard Cream

1 cup each milk and light cream, mixed
1 cup whipped cream
¾ cup sugar
4 egg yolks, well beaten
2 tblspns each butter and cornstarch
1½ tsp vanilla
pinch salt

1. In the top of a double boiler, combine the sugar, cornstarch and salt. Stir in, gradually, the milk and cream mixture and then cook, covered, over boiling water for 6-8 minutes without stirring. Uncover and continue to cook 10 minutes longer. Add the egg yolks and butter, stirring over the heat for an additional 2 minutes.

2. Allow to cool for 15-20 minutes, stirring occasionally. Add the vanilla and fold in the whipped cream. Refrigerate and serve well chilled.

Serves 6.

Chocolate Custard

2 cups light cream
½ lb (225 gr) sweet chocolate
6 egg yolks, lightly beaten
2 tblspns sugar
1 tsp vanilla

1. In a saucepan over a very low flame, combine and cook the cream, chocolate and sugar, stirring well until ingredients are melted and cream is barely bubbling at the edges. Remove from heat and beat in the remaining ingredients. Strain into individual cups, refrigerate and serve well chilled.

Serves 6.

Baked Apples with Pineapple

6 large apples for cooking
6 slices canned pineapple
¼ cup sugar
1 ½ tsp cinnamon
2 oz (56 gr) butter

1. Core apples and remove the flesh leaving the shells intact. Chop the flesh coarsely.
2. Mix the chopped apple flesh with the sugar. Fill the apple shells and place butter pats on each apple. Sprinkle each with cinnamon.
3. Lay the pineapple slices in a lightly greased baking dish. On each slice set one filled apple. Put in hot oven for 15 minutes. Serve hot. Excellent served with sweetened whipped cream.

Serves 6.

Apple-Prune Compote

2 cups prunes
1 ½ cups dried apples
1 ¼ cups sugar
rind of 1 large lemon

1. In a large mixing bowl soak the apples and prunes with water to cover for 1-2 hours. Drain. Combine all ingredients in a saucepan with 6 cups cold water. Bring to a boil and then lower flame and cover. Simmer over low flame 15-20 minutes. Remove fruit with a slotted spoon and place in serving bowl.
2. Simmer the liquid, half covered, over low flame ½ hour. Allow to cool 15-20 minutes and then pour over the fruit. Refrigerate, covered, until chilled. Serve well chilled.

Serves 6.

Fruit Compote

½ lb (225 gr) each dried apricots, apples and prunes
¾ cup sugar
2 tblspns lemon juice

1. Soak the dry fruit in 6 cups water for 1½-2 hours. Bring to a boil and then add the sugar and lemon juice. Stir well, lower the flame and let simmer, covered, for 45 minutes, or until tender. Refrigerate, covered, and serve cold with the liquid.

Serves 6.

Prunes with Almonds

1 lb (450 gr) prunes, pitted
2 oz (56 gr) almonds, peeled and chopped
2 oz (56 gr) seedless raisins
2 cups dry red wine
½ cup sugar
3 whole cloves
1½ tsp cinnamon

1. In a saucepan mix the prunes, almonds, raisins, cloves, wine, cinnamon and sugar. Bring the mixture to a boil stirring constantly. Lower the flame and continue cooking and stirring while mixture thickens. Remove cloves and serve hot.

Serves 4-6.

Pears in Red Wine

12 large pears
1 bottle dry red wine
1 cup plus 8 tsp sugar
2 lemons, sliced
4 whole cloves

1. Halve the pears lengthwise and remove cores. Arrange in a single layer in a baking dish.

143

2. In a saucepan mix the wine, cloves, 1 cup sugar and ¼ cup water. Heat until wine begins to simmer and pour over the pears. Sprinkle ¼ tsp sugar over each pear half. Arrange the lemon slices over the pears. Place in medium oven for 20 minutes.

3. Remove from oven, turn pears and sprinkle ¼ tsp sugar onto the second side. Return to oven until pears are done. Cover and cool in refrigerator. Serve cold. May be served with sweetened whipped cream.

Serves 6 or 12.

Baked Pears with Nuts

4 large pears, peeled, cored and halved
½ cup light corn syrup
½ cup seedless raisins
½ cup pineapple juice
2 tblspns each sugar and chopped walnuts
2 tblspns brown sugar
1 tblspn lemon juice

1. Mix together the raisins, nuts, sugar and lemon juice, and with this fill the hollows of the pear halves. Place the filled halves in an oven casserole with 2 - 3 tblspns water and over the halves pour the syrup.

2. Combine the pineapple juice and brown sugar.

3. Bake the pears in a medium oven for 1 ½ hours, basting during the baking with the pineapple juice mixture. Serve hot.

Serves 4.

The Intellectual in the Cafeteria

A merry heart maketh a cheerful countenance.
Proverbs 15:13

AT LEAST since the time of the Pharaohs, people have tried to understand what it was that made Jews "different". Many scholars have speculated that it was love for Torah that set Jews apart, but this is only partly accurate. It is not that one should diminish the enormous role of Torah, which taken in its broadest context includes not only the Five Books of Moses but the entire Bible and oral law together with history, legend, folklore and moral and ethical teachings. While this may have given Jews their basic outlook on life, there are two particular traits, derived perhaps from Torah, which when taken together best describe Jews as a people. The two, inseparable, are optimism and inquisitiveness.

Optimism is an integral part of Judaism. Even in the most excruciatingly difficult times the people maintained the attitude that the world would become better. This hope for a better tomorrow has been a powerful force in the continuation of the people collectively and of Jews individually. Poverty was always viewed as something temporary; persecution and oppression as phenomena that would pass. Life, despite its trials, was a gift, always to be prized; the world, with all its foibles, was basically a good place.

The second trait, inquisitiveness, is no less important to being Jewish. For Jews, absolutely everything is open to question. And more: everything *must* be questioned. There is no issue, whether of faith or daily pragmatic events, that is taken as fixed forever. Nothing can be taken fully for granted if it is to be fully appreciated; there are no issues that have been forever resolved.

The two traits, when combined, form an attitude which implies that one must, no matter how pressed the day or circumstance, make time in which to both enjoy and discuss life. Nor is it enough to take such moments only alone. There must be, in addition to the hours stolen during the day, a special time to celebrate — to sit at leisure with at least one other soul in order to share the moment.

For the hard-pressed peasant, the banker, the intellectual and even at such terrible places as Birkinau or Auschwitz, Jews have always made such time. It has been part of what allowed their survival, their dignity and their joy.

There are several specifics to the habit. Such pleasures are invariably accompanied by a glass of tea, coffee or schnapps; whether at home or in public they take on an air of great leisure; and the discussions are, by seeming pre-arrangement, lively and controversial. In the shtetls of eastern Europe such meetings took place either in the homes of the people or in local inns that chanced to serve beverages; in European cities they took place in the cafes. It was left to the New World to develop the concept of the cafeteria where such activities were raised to their ultimate art-form.

The particular places that happened to become favourite haunts were neither pretentious nor extravagant. The daily excursion into the world of such pleasures was, to a great extent, a return to one's past, to simpler roots.

More than a few continue with the habit today. Friends are still met regularly for coffee and long talks; coffee and tea are still to be drunk from a glass and not a cup at such meetings; if one drinks tea it is not by spooning in the sugar but by holding a small sugar cube in a corner of the mouth to be dissolved with each leisurely sip. If it is a morning meeting the traditional snack, always to accompany the tea, is a soft roll, ideally with a bit of butter; in the early afternoon coffee cakes or cookies suffice handsomely; and for the evening there are fine cakes. The cakes are not really important. What *is* important is the beverage, the companionship, the discussion and the at least momentary freedom in which to enjoy those.

Equally important is the ability, the time, the very act of sitting with one's feet comfortably spread, taking an occasional sip of tea and taking part in the debate of the moment. The most exquisite moments are not those, however, that are associated with the tea, the friends or the words. These are the moments that come, if only briefly, to remind us that there is indeed beauty in the world, that tomorrow will bring a better day and that even though all may not be well, it may be made better. At such moments, such escapes from the real day, whether one believes in the existence of God or not, one gives very grateful thanks for the tea, the roll, perhaps the bit of butter, and for the friend with whom one sits. And that one is there.

D.G.

Egg Cookies — Kichelech

3 cups self-rising flour
5 eggs, well beaten
8 tblspns butter, melted
2½ tblspns sugar

1. Blend together the eggs, melted butter and sugar. To this gradually add the flour and knead well on a well-floured board (about 5 minutes). Roll out dough on floured board to ⅛" (¼ cm) thickness and cut into rounds. Transfer the individual cookies to a greased cookie sheet and bake in medium oven until golden (about 30 minutes).

Yields about 36 cookies.

Humentashen

A special treat usually reserved for the holiday of Purim. Called *osnei haman* (Haman's ears) in Hebrew, these are specially tasty when munched along with a glass of tea, milk or coffee.

The Dough

2½ cups flour
¾ cup milk
½ cup sugar
1 egg, lightly beaten
6 tblspns melted butter
2½ tsp baking powder
½ tsp salt
filling of choice (following recipes)

1. Combine the flour, baking powder, sugar and salt, mixing well. Add the melted butter, egg and milk and mix again. On a floured board knead well and then roll out to ⅛″ (¼ cm) thickness. Cut out rounds about 2½″ (6 cm) in diameter.
2. Onto the centre of each round place 1 heaping tsp of the filling (see below). Pinch together three sides of the round to form a triangle and place individually-formed cookies on a greased cookie sheet. Bake in medium oven until cookies are golden brown (25-30 minutes).

Yields about 30 cookies.

Fillings for Humentashen

Nut and Raisin Filling

1 cup raisins
1 cup chopped walnuts
⅓ cup chopped almonds
⅓ cup brown sugar
⅓ cup orange juice
rind of 1 orange
rind of ½ lemon
1 tsp cinnamon
½ tsp ground cloves

1. Combine all ingredients in a saucepan and cook over low flame, stirring constantly, until the mixture is moist and cohesive.

Date Filling

4 cups chopped dates
1 cup chopped walnuts
½ cup dry or sweet red wine
4 tblspns butter
3 tsp cinnamon

1. Place dates, wine and butter in a small saucepan. Cook over low heat, stirring constantly, for 8 - 10 minutes until mixture is pastelike. Allow to cool 10 minutes and stir in the cinnamon and nuts.

Prune Filling

1 cup prunes, pitted
1 cup milk
½ cup sugar
¼ cup ground poppy seeds
2½ tblspns butter, melted
1 tsp vanilla

1. Soak prunes in water to cover 2½ - 3 hours. Drain and chop finely. Combine all ingredients, except vanilla, in a saucepan and cook, stirring frequently, over low flame until the mixture thickens (about 20 minutes). Allow to cool 15 - 20 minutes and stir in the vanilla.

Raisin and Nut Filling

1¼ cups seedless raisins
1 cup milk
½ cup ground poppy seeds
½ cup chopped walnuts
½ cup sugar
3 tblspns melted butter
1 tsp vanilla

1. Soak raisins in water to cover 1½ - 2 hours. Drain and chop finely. Combine all ingredients, except vanilla, in a saucepan and cook, stirring frequently, over low flame until the mixture thickens (about 20 minutes). Allow to cool 15 - 20 minutes and stir in the vanilla.

Poppy Seed Filling

⅔ cup poppy seeds
½ cup milk
½ cup sugar
¼ cup dried bread crumbs
¼ cup chopped raisins
3 tblspns honey
juice and rind of 1 lemon

1. In a heavy saucepan bring the milk and sugar to a boil and immediately reduce to low flame. Add poppy seeds and continue cooking, stirring constantly, until mixture thickens. Remove from heat and stir in remaining ingredients.

Each mixture yields enough filling for about 30 cookies.

Macaroon Cookies

2 cups coconut flakes
3 egg whites, room temperature
1 cup sugar
1 tblspn lemon juice

1. Whip egg whites until stiff enough to form peaks. To these add the sugar, 1 tblspn at a time, whipping for 1 - 1½ minutes after each addition. When sugar is dissolved continue whipping 5 minutes longer while gradually adding in the lemon juice.

2. On this meringue sprinkle the coconut a little at a time and fold in gently.

3. Prepare a cookie tin by greasing lightly with shortening. On this lay a sheet of waxed paper and grease this as well. Onto the waxed paper form small mounds of batter. Bake in low oven for 20 minutes, and then open oven door, turn heat off and allow to stand another 20 minutes. Cool before carefully peeling the individual cookies from the paper.

Yields about 24 - 30 cookies.

Coffee Cake with Raisins

4 cups flour, sifted
1 cup each milk and butter, softened
1 cup seedless raisins
¾ cup sugar
½ cup blanched almonds
6 eggs
3 cakes compressed yeast, crumbled
1 tsp salt
1 tsp grated lemon rind
confectioners' sugar

1. Before starting, be certain that all ingredients and utensils are at room temperature.
2. In a saucepan heat the milk until bubbles begin to appear at the edges. Remove from heat and allow to cool to nearly room temperature. Pour this over the yeast and allow to stand until yeast has dissolved. Beat in 1 cup of the flour and allow to rise in a warm place until about double in bulk.
3. Sift the sugar and add this slowly to the butter, blending together until creamlike. To this beat in, one at a time, the eggs and then the salt. To this add the yeast-flour mixture, the remaining flour, lemon rind and raisins. Beat the batter thoroughly until smooth and elastic.
4. In the bottom of a greased 9" (22 cm) tube pan, spread the almonds and on top of them place the dough. Allow to rise again until almost double in bulk. Bake in medium oven until done (about 50 - 60 minutes or until a sharp knife blade comes out clean). Allow to cool and sprinkle with confectioners' sugar.

Yields 1 cake.

Kupferlin

2 cups flour, sifted
1 cup salted margarine
½ cup sugar
½ cup almonds, ground finely
confectioners' sugar

1. Cream together the margarine and sugar. Add the almonds and then the

flour. Mixing by hand, knead well.

2. Taking balls of flour about 2″ (5 cm) in diameter, roll each into tube-shaped pieces about 2″ (5 cm) long, and then shape each piece into a semi-circle. Place these on an ungreased cookie sheet and bake for 40 minutes in very low (250°F or 120°C) oven. When done cookies should be white in colour and not at all browned. Remove from oven, let stand 15-20 minutes and then sprinkle with confectioners' sugar.

Yields about 24 cookies.

Kuchen

For most European Jews, kuchen is a flat sugar-cake, cookie-like in nature, part of the pleasure in which is breaking off small bits by hand and munching with coffee, with tea or with absolutely nothing. Kuchen dough may also be used to make roll-like cakes and serves excellently as pastry backings for apple or other fruit fillings.

The Dough

5 cups flour, sifted
1 cup butter, soft
1 cup scalded milk
¾ cup sugar
¼ cup milk, lukewarm
1 envelope dry active yeast
2 eggs, well beaten
1¼ tsp salt

1. Dissolve the yeast in the lukewarm milk, add 1 tblspn sugar, cover and set aside for 5-10 minutes.
2. Combine the scalded milk with the remaining sugar and salt. Add the butter and stir well until butter is melted and evenly distributed. Set aside to cool, and then combine the yeast mixture and the butter and milk mixture. Into this slowly sift the flour, mixing regularly until the dough is smooth and pliable. Place the dough on a lightly floured board and knead for 5 minutes. Shape into a ball, transfer to a bowl and cover with a damp cloth. Let rise in warm place until the volume doubles.

To prepare Kuchen cookies:

1. After the dough has doubled in volume, punch down and spread on a lightly greased cookie tin so that dough is about ⅛" (¼ cm) thick. Cover again with damp cloth and let rise in a warm place until doubled in thickness. Place the cookie tin in a medium oven and bake until top is golden brown (about 20-25 minutes). Allow kuchen to cool and then break into convenient pieces.

Kuchen Rollada

kuchen dough (preceding page)
1 cup seedless raisins
½ cup brown sugar
½ cup butter, melted
4 tsp cinnamon

1. Follow steps 1 and 2 in the making of kuchen dough (see preceding page). After the kuchen dough has doubled in volume, punch down and place on lightly greased surface. Roll out to ¼" (½ cm) thickness and brush with half the melted butter.
2. Mix the brown sugar, cinnamon and raisins together. Distribute this evenly over the dough. Roll up the dough and divide the roll into two even lengths. Place each roll in a well greased tube pan, cover with damp cloth and let rise in warm place until volume has again doubled. Brush the cakes with the remainder of the melted butter and bake in moderate oven until top is well browned (about 30-35 minutes).

Yields 2 cakes.

Kuchen Fruit Cake

kuchen dough (preceding page)
9 sour apples, peeled, cored and sliced
*   or 9 pears, peeled, cored and sliced*
*   or 1½ lbs (675 gr) dried apricots*
6 tblspns brown sugar
¼ lb (115 gr) butter
3 tsp cinnamon

1. Follow steps 1 and 2 in the making of kuchen dough (see page 152). After the dough has doubled in volume, punch down and separate into 3 equal parts. Spread each part in a lightly greased 9″ (22 cm) pie tin, covering bottom and sides equally.
2. Place the fruit slices into the dough in neat rows. Mix the sugar and cinnamon and sprinkle over the fruit. Dot with butter, cover with damp cloth and let rise in warm place until doubled in bulk. Bake in moderate oven until golden brown (about 20-25 minutes).

Yields 3 cakes.

Shabbes Honey Cake

This cake should be prepared several days before serving in order for flavour and texture to be ideal. Because it requires no cooking on the day it is served, it proves ideal for the Sabbath.

2½ cups flour, sifted
¾ cup honey
⅔ cup brown sugar
½ cup very strong black coffee
4 eggs, separated
1¾ tsp baking powder
¾ tsp baking soda
½ tsp each salt, allspice, ground cloves

1. In a large mixing bowl combine the egg yolks and sugar and beat until creamy. Add the oil to the mixture and beat well and then add the honey, beating again until the mixture is creamy and smooth.
2. Combine the sifted flour, baking powder, baking soda and spices. Add the dry ingredients to the honey mixture alternately with the coffee, stirring with wooden spoon, until ingredients are well blended.
3. Beat the egg whites stiff and fold gently into the batter. Pour the batter into a lightly greased baking pan (8-cup capacity) and bake in low oven for about 1½ hours. The cake is done when a dry knife comes out dry and clean. Let cool and cover with plastic wrap. Let stand 2-3 days before serving.

Passover Sponge Cake

½ cup matzo meal
1 cup sugar
6 eggs, room temperature, separated
4 tblspns potato starch
1 tblspn oil
juice of 1 lemon
rind from 1 lemon, grated
½ tsp salt

1. Sift together the matzo meal and potato starch.
2. Combine the egg yolks, oil and lemon juice, whipping until thick and lemon coloured.
3. Whip the egg whites with the salt until peaks form. Add the sugar, 1 tblspn at a time, beating well after each addition.
4. Add the egg yolk mixture to the beaten egg white mixture folding in gently with a wooden spatula. Fold in the dry ingredients a little at a time. Add in the grated lemon rind and fold into the batter. Pour batter into a lightly greased 10″ (25 cm) pan and gently spread the batter so that it is even. Bake in medium oven about 40 minutes. The cake is finished when a sharp knife blade comes out dry and clean. Cool before removing from pan.

Yields 1 cake.

Cheesecake

1½ cups sour cream
1½ cups graham cracker crumbs
1¼ cups sugar
1 lb (450 gr) cream cheese
6 tblspns butter, melted
2 eggs
1½ tsp vanilla

1. Combine the crumbs and melted butter and press this crust over the bottom of a deep 9″ (22 cm) pie plate. Mix the cream cheese, sugar, vanilla and eggs and pour this over the crumb base. Bake in low oven 25 minutes. Cool for 10-15 minutes.

2. Combine the remaining ingredients and pour these over the top of the cake. Bake for 15 minutes longer. Cool for 10 - 15 minutes before covering lightly and refrigerating. Serve well chilled.

Serves 6 - 8.

Chanukah Doughnuts — Soofganiot

This particular doughnut is a Mediterranean specialty and is claimed by the Greeks, Turks, Spanish, French, North Africans and Israelis as their own. In Israel they are especially popular at Chanukah but wise men and women know that they can be eaten at any time of the year.

3 cups flour
¼ lb (115 gr) butter or margarine, melted
1 oz (30 gr) active dry yeast
2 egg yolks
6 tblspns sugar
confectioners' sugar as needed
1 ½ tsp brandy or bourbon
oil for deep frying

1. Combine the yeast and 1 tblspn each of sugar, flour and warm water. Cover with a towel and let stand until it rises.
2. In a separate mixing bowl, combine the flour, melted butter, brandy, salt, sugar and egg yolks. Mix well and then add the yeast mixture, mixing well again. To this mixture slowly add between 1¼ - 1½ cups of warm water, stirring until batter is smooth. Cover the batter with a towel and set aside to rise.
3. After the batter has risen turn it onto a well-floured board. Cover the mixture with a towel and flatten by hand. Using an inverted wine glass (or other similar in size) punch individual pieces from the dough. Cover these and let rise once again.
4. Drop the individual pieces in a large pot with very hot deep oil and fry until both sides are brown, turning the doughnuts occasionally as they fry. Remove doughnuts with a slotted spoon and over each sprinkle confectioners' sugar. Serve hot or at room temperature.

Yields about 20 doughnuts.

Soofganiot Filled with Jam

4 cups flour
½ cup sugar
¼ cup oil
2 envelopes dry active yeast
1 egg, lightly beaten
¾ tsp salt
jam for filling
confectioners' sugar as needed
oil for deep frying

1. Combine the yeast and 2 tblspns each of sugar, flour and warm water. Cover with a towel and let stand until it rises.
2. In a separate mixing bowl, combine the flour, oil, salt, sugar and eggs. Mix well and add 1 cup warm water and the yeast mixture. Stir until batter is smooth and firm. Cover the batter with a towel and set aside to rise until doubled in bulk (about 30 minutes).
3. After the batter has risen turn it onto a well-floured board. Beat down dough, cover with damp towel and allow to rise again. Cover the mixture with a towel and flatten by hand. Using an inverted wine glass (or other similar in size) cut out individual pieces from the dough. Cover these and allow to rise once again, for about ½ hour.
4. Drop the individual pieces in a large pot with very hot deep oil and fry until both sides are brown, turning the doughnuts occasionally as they fry. Remove with a slotted spoon and drain on absorbent paper. Using a cake decorator with jam, fill the inside of each doughnut. Sprinkle with confectioners' sugar. Serve hot or at room temperature.

Yields about 24 doughnuts.

Pontchekes

These deep-fried mini doughnuts are ideal when served with toothpicks so that they may be dipped into honey or warmed maple syrup.

2 cups flour
10 eggs
½ lb (225 gr) sweet butter
pinch salt
oil for deep frying

1. In a large skillet bring 1 cup water to a boil. Add the butter and continue boiling, stirring constantly until the butter is melted. Add the salt and flour and mix with wooden spoon until the mixture forms a dough ball. Remove from flame.
2. Beat in the eggs 2 at a time making sure that each egg is completely absorbed into the mixture before adding others.
3. In a large saucepan with deep hot oil drop in the dough a teaspoon at a time. Allow balls to puff and turn occasionally. Remove from oil with slotted spoon and drain on paper towelling. Serve hot with honey or warmed maple syrup.

Yields about 36 pontchekes.

Fruit Cake

The holiday of *Tu Bishvat* (literally the 15th day of the Hebrew month of Shvat) celebrates the onset of spring, the new year of the trees and the recycling of the earth. It is traditional in Israel to plant saplings on this day and for Jews the world over to celebrate by serving fruits and nuts — especially those that are borne by trees. This cake is well suited to the holiday.

2½ cups flour
¼ cup each dried dates, figs, apricots and apples, all diced
¾ cup brown sugar
⅓ cup walnuts or pecans, chopped
4 tblspns butter
1 egg
2 tsp baking powder
1¼ tsp baking soda

1. In a large mixing bowl combine the brown sugar, butter and egg, mixing well. To this add 1 cup lukewarm water and mix until ingredients are well blended. Sift into this mixture the flour, baking powder and baking soda. Mix well, and then add the diced fruits, again mixing well.
2. Place the batter in a very well-greased loaf pan. Let stand 15-20 minutes and bake in a medium oven for about 1 hour. Cake will be done when a sharp knife blade comes out clean and dry. Remove from pan and cool.

Yields 1 cake.

Mandel Broit

4 cups flour
¼ lb (115 gr) butter
1 cup sugar
3 eggs, well beaten
2 tsp baking powder
2 tsp vegetable shortening
1 tsp each vanilla and almond extracts
pinch baking soda

1. Mix the sugar, butter and shortening and cream well.
2. Mix together the flour, baking powder and baking soda.
3. Add the eggs and dry ingredients alternately to the creamed mixture. Add the vanilla and almond extracts and mix well. Mould the dough into four equal balls. Roll out each ball and flatten on greased cookie sheet. Bake in medium oven until beginning to brown. Remove from oven and slice each sheet. Turn individual pieces on their sides and return to oven until brown. Turn and brown other side, taking care not to burn.

Apple Strudel

2½ cups flour, sifted
4 large sour apples, peeled, cored and grated
½ lb (225 gr) butter, softened
½ cup seedless raisins
½ cup almonds, ground
8 tblspns dried bread crumbs
3 tblspns honey
2 tblspns sugar
2 tblspns oil
1 tsp each vinegar and cinnamon
¼ tsp salt
1 egg
confectioners' sugar

1. In a large mixing bowl cut the butter into the flour. By hand, crumble the butter in the flour until at the consistency of cornmeal. Combine in a cup ½ cup cold water, the vinegar and salt and sprinkle this over the flour. Blend

together and then, by hand, knead 40-50 times. After the dough has become elastic beat it well by hand and then shape into 2 equal balls. Cover these with a damp towel and let stand 1 hour in refrigerator.

2. On a well-floured board roll out the dough balls into rectangles about 12 × 15" (30 × 40 cm).

3. Prepare the filling by combining the apples, sugar, honey, raisins, almonds, cinnamon and 5 tblspns of the bread crumbs. Mix well.

4. Brush each of the dough rectangles with 1 tblspn oil and then divide the filling over them. Spread the filling so that it is evenly distributed. Roll the rectangles length-wise (as in a jelly roll).

5. Transfer the strudels to a lightly greased cookie sheet and place them on the pan with the fold underneath. Pinch together the open edges and tuck them in.

6. Combine the egg with 2 tblspns water and beat well. With this brush the tops of the strudels. Make 1" (2½ cm) diagonal cuts in the tops of the strudels, spaced at 1" (2½ cm) intervals and bake in medium oven until nicely browned (about 1 hour). Cool and sprinkle with confectioners' sugar.

Yields 2 strudels.

Chocolate Cake — Babke

2½ cups flour, sifted
½ cup lukewarm milk
½ cup sugar
¼ cup butter, softened
¼ cup seedless raisins
4 oz (115 gr) bittersweet chocolate
2 eggs, well beaten
1½ tblspns very strong black coffee
1 tblspn butter, melted
½ envelope active dry yeast
¼ tsp salt

1. Dissolve the yeast in 1 tblspn of the milk and let stand for 5-10 minutes.

2. Into a large mixing bowl, sift ½ cup flour, ¼ cup sugar and the salt. Stir in the remaining milk, add the yeast mixture and mix well. Cover with a damp cloth and set aside in warm place for about 45 minutes.

3. Cream together the butter with the remaining sugar and add this to the dough mixture. Blend in the eggs. Sift in the remaining flour and mix until smooth. (Add flour if necessary to ensure a smooth, pliable mixture.)

4. Over a double boiler melt the chocolate and then stir in the coffee and raisins.

5. On a lightly floured board spread the dough and coat with the chocolate mixture. Roll the dough over until a multi-layered roll has been formed. Place the roll in a well-greased baking pan, cover with damp cloth and let rise in a warm place until the volume is doubled. Brush the top with the melted butter and bake in a medium oven 40 minutes.

Yields 1 cake.

Afterword

MOGILEV IS A small city in the region alternatively known as White or Belorussia. It sits on the Dnieper River and is just a bit closer to Minsk than to Pinsk. It is not far from the ravine known as Babi Yar. Although Yiddish culture neither started nor ended in Mogilev, there may be no better place to seek an understanding of how Jews lived in the old country, how some of them perished and how many of them left for newer worlds.

Until half a century ago Mogilev was a comfortable village, the population being composed of peasants, tradespeople and craftsmen. Even though there were a few professionals and some of the others had spent a year or two at university, it was a simple place to live. The Jews and Christians of the village lived together comfortably and Mogilev had been just a bit too far off the beaten track to have made pogroms convenient.

The streets were neat but unpaved, the houses ranged from one to six rooms in size and it was an overall attractive community. There were several orthodox families but most of the Jews might have been better described as "traditional" rather than as "religious". Some members of the Jewish community belonged to the communist party as did others of the townspeople, but the atmosphere was one of quiet reform rather than of revolution.

There were two rabbis, two synagogues and a ritual slaughterer. There were even several Hassidic Jews in town. Most of the Jews spoke Yiddish at home but Russian on the streets. Even the poorest home did not suffer from a lack of food, for although there was no specific air of charity in Mogilev, there was a sense of community and of sharing.

The first wave of Jews left Mogilev starting in 1904, when the Tsar entered into the Russo-Japanese war and conscripted Jews to send to that far-away front. Many of the men left before conscription, others deserted after they had been taken into the army and realized that they were merely being sent to die. Those who left went either to Palestine or to New York. It depended more on where one had relatives than on questions of idealism. Once they settled in they sent for their families. A minority stayed on and life continued smoothly. They were Jews but they were Russians as well and they felt at home. It remained good until 1941 when the Nazis came.

The Jews of Mogilev were not deported nor were they sent to the camps. They were simply taken to the town square and machine-gunned.

A few escaped. Some seventeen people travelling primarily by foot for over two years finally reached ports where, with forged papers and bribe money, they boarded ships. They had wanted to go to Palestine but that was not then possible, so it was in New York City that they finally found themselves. By 1943 there were nearly as many Jews who had originated in Mogilev living in New York as there had been in Mogilev itself.

And the Russian village had taken, in its way, new roots in America. Although the immigrants lived in the Bronx, in Brooklyn and in Manhattan, they met often. Whether it was to sip tea, drink schnapps or to play gin rummy they were, in many ways, a family. Oscar Joroff had founded the Mogilev on Dnieper Benevolent Association, a group dedicated to helping lantzmen who had found their way either to America or to Palestine. He had also founded the Mogilev on Dnieper Mashiv Skanim (from Hebrew, *moshav zkaneem*, or community for the aged).

Those who arrived in the '40s found a style of life that was simultaneously a public and private re-creation of Mogilev's ethics, comfort and ease together with an adaptation to the ways of America. Neighbours were still important, friends were valued and honoured, and Jewish tradition continued to play a major role for the people.

The Russian language had been replaced by English but Yiddish was still spoken in the homes and at the meetings of Modba (as the children and grandchildren came to know the Benevolent Association). Aunts and uncles, real or adopted, came to visit on weekends and the world was comfortable once again.

The grandparents grew old and died; most of the parents are by now either very old or already dead. The children now have children and even grandchildren of their own. Most are not particularly religious but remain devotedly Jewish in their ways. Yiddish is rarely spoken but the words and phrases are remembered and used frequently to spice the now native English. Many continue to light candles on the Sabbath, and most attend synagogue during the holidays. Their children are Bar or Bat Mitzvah and, if they belong to synagogues at all, it is the Reform Movement that attracts them.

Modba now exists only as a burial society, and nearly all of those who originally came from Mogilev have used their services. There are only a few who remember. And when they do, it is with joy for what was, with tears for what came to pass, with pride that they were part of it and with gratefulness that they have survived to write about it.

D.R.